THE SYDING ADVENTURES
ROMANS
AND
RANSOMS
WRITTEN BY
4
MARY WEEKS MILLARD
TELEPHONE
DayOne

First printed 2014

ISBN 978-1-84625-367-6

All Scripture quotations are from the **New International Version** 1984
Copyright © 1973, 1978, 1984

Published by Day One Publications
Ryelands Road, Leominster, HR6 8NZ

TEL 01568 613 740 FAX 01568 611 473

email—sales@dayone.co.uk

UK web site—www.dayone.co.uk

This book is entirely a work of fiction. Some actual place names have been used, but the names of all people and the villages where they live are entirely fictitious.

Printed by TJ International

Dedication

To Lucy Jane

I hope you enjoy this book when you are a little older. I am grateful to your daddy for reading some of the books in this series.

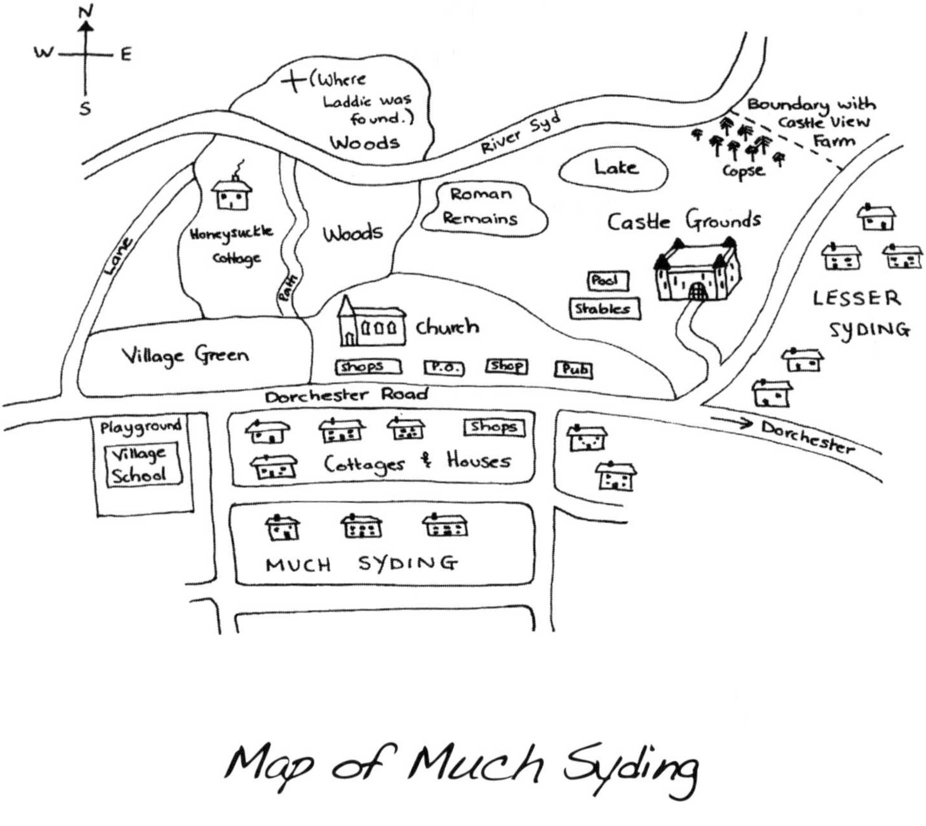

Map of Much Syding

Acknowledgments

My thanks as always to Tirzah Jones, Youth Director of DayOne, for her encouragement and to Chris Jones for her sensitive editing and all DayOne staff involved in the production of this book.

My grateful thanks to Ella Vellacott and Bradley Styles for reading this book and writing endorsements.

My thanks to my husband, Malcolm, for all his support and encouragement and my family for their interest.

Chapter One

Tess was very, very excited. It was a cold February morning and the mist was swirling around the farm. Everywhere looked damp and grey, but Tess was happy. Today was her ninth birthday! She sang softly to herself as she washed and dressed. She could hear the milking machine working in the cowshed and hoped that her dad would be finished in time for breakfast. Often Tess and her brothers, Tim and Paul, didn't see their dad until late in the evening. Farming was hard work, and he only had some part time help at the moment.

When Tess reached the big farmhouse kitchen, she found all the family sitting around the table waiting for her! Her mum started to sing, 'Happy birthday to you,' and everyone joined in. Tess could feel her cheeks going pink with pleasure. Where her plate should have been were a pile of parcels!

"Open them quickly, Tess," said her big brother Paul, "because I have to catch the school bus."

Paul was at the senior school in the nearby market town of Dorchester, and the school bus stopped at the farm gate to pick him up. If he missed it, it would be a long cycle ride, and he would be late and get a detention.

Tess began to open the parcels. Paul had bought her a tin of water colour pencils of every shade imaginable! She was so thrilled, because although she struggled with almost every subject at school, she excelled in art. To go with the pencils, her other brother Tim, who was ten and a half, had bought her a large pad of drawing paper. There were other gifts to open: a bag from her granny and grandad, some story books from her aunt and uncle and a necklace from her other grandparents. She had so many pretty cards too, which she placed on show on the Welsh dresser.

"Your present from daddy and me is in the hall," said Mum with a big smile. Tess got up and ran into the hallway and there, with a big pink bow, was a bike! It was silver and purple and was fantastic!

"Thank you, thank you!" she exclaimed and ran to give her parents each a big hug. She had grown out of her old bike ages ago and every time she rode it, her knees hit the handle bars. This one was amazing!

"Can I ride it to school?" asked Tess.

"Not until the summer," answered her dad. "It's still too dark in the mornings, but after school when the clocks change, you can. That gives you lots of time to practice and get used to riding it around the farm."

"Right everyone, birthday or not, you must be off to school. Run and get your things," Mum said to Tim and

Tess. They were driven to the primary school in the village of Much Syding, a couple of miles away.

It was a small school, and because of this the pupils all knew each other quite well. Several of the girls came up to Tess and wished her a happy birthday, and her best friend Kayla gave her a card and a big bag of marshmallows, her favourite sweet. She told Kayla all about her new shiny purple and silver bike and that in the spring she would be able to ride it to school. Kayla was coming home with her after school for a birthday tea, so she would be able to see it, and maybe they would be able to ride around the farm yard until it got dark. Kayla was also nine and had been at Much Syding School since the previous September. She was very quiet and shy, but very clever at her lessons. She loved going to visit Tess at the farm because she had no brothers or sisters and her mother was allergic to animal fur, so there were no pets allowed at her house. When she visited the farm, Kayla loved to see the animals and also feel the buzz and friendliness of Tess and her family as well as their friends who often seemed to be there. She loved her parents dearly, but they were always working, and so she had to amuse herself most of the time. She knew her father was very clever, a scientist, although she did not know exactly what he did. Her mother spent most of her time in her study, writing articles for magazines. She always seemed to have a 'deadline' to meet. Kayla had a beautiful room, all pink and mauve and very pretty. She spent hours on her bed reading books. Her parents had a library with shelves of books, and one section was full of story books. Kayla loved them! Her parents and school friends called her a 'book worm', but she didn't mind.

When school was finished for the day, Tess and Tim waited for their mum to come to meet them and Kayla. It was still misty and cold, so riding around the farm yard wasn't really a good idea, but the girls did have a couple of rounds each. Kayla was a bit wobbly on a bike because she didn't have one of her own, but she soon got the hang of it. Then Tess took her to see the new lambs. There were four in the barn who were orphaned and needed to be bottle fed and to her great delight, Kayla was able to help with this.

Everyone in the area knew that Mrs Jenkins was a fine cook, and what a spread she had made for Tess's birthday tea! The birthday cake was very special and was in the shape of a bicycle. Everyone was amazed and wondered how she had managed to make it! It tasted wonderful and soon didn't look like a bike any more!

After tea the girls watched a Disney DVD which Tess had been given by an auntie. It was lovely sitting by the roaring log fire and laughing together. The time went so quickly Kayla was surprised when she heard her father's voice coming from the kitchen. He had arrived to take her home.

She thanked Mrs Jenkins for such a lovely time and was just about to get into the car when Paul came rushing up.

"Mum," he said breathlessly, "Pickles is having her puppies!"

Pickles was a golden Labrador, adored by the children. They began to rush over to the barn, Kayla and her father following behind.

"I doubt that Pickles will need my help," remarked Mrs Jenkins. "She is a very good mother!"

"Fancy them being born on my birthday!" said Tess. "What a nice present, Pickles!"

There were four strong wriggly puppies and one tiny one that was struggling to breathe.

"That is the runt," Kayla's dad explained to her. "He will need a lot of care if he is to make it."

Mrs Jenkins was rubbing him in a towel and helping him. "I think we had better call him 'Omega' as he is the last!" she commented.

"Why?" asked Tess. "What does Omega mean?"

Her friend answered before Mrs Jenkins could get her breath. "It's the last letter of the Greek alphabet, so it means 'The end'."

Tim and Paul looked at Kayla in amazement. Fancy her knowing the Greek alphabet.

Chapter Two

Tim was looking forward to Saturday. The Wildlife Society was meeting at Syding Castle. Usually he had very little to say at the meetings, and although he didn't find them boring, they weren't exactly exciting either to him. He really much preferred cars, tractors or anything mechanical. He couldn't wait until his father thought he was old enough to drive the farm tractor. He adored going out in the Land Rover and always helped his dad to clean it and hung around when he was fixing it. Tim knew every car in both villages and could recognize most of them just by their engine noises.

He knew what he wanted to be when he was grown up—a car mechanic. He thought wildlife was nowhere near so interesting, but he had kept his nature diary along with the others and liked being part of the club. This time though, he was pleased because he had seen something which he had not seen before. At least, Tim didn't think he had. Maybe it was just that he had never taken much notice before of the animals and plants around him. Certainly belonging to the club had made him notice much more.

Saturday morning was bright and sunny, even though the temperature was only just above freezing. Living on a farm meant that there were jobs which had to be done before the children were free to go to the castle. Tim's job was to clean the cars. Dad had driven the Land Rover and also his mum's Volvo Estate into the main farm yard so that he could hose them down.

"Don't spend too long at it today," advised his dad. "It is so cold, I don't want you to freeze!"

"Ok, Dad," Tim answered cheerily as he put on his wellies and an old anorak.

Paul was helping to feed the pigs, while Tess was in the barn bottle feeding the orphaned lambs.

When they had all finished, they went into the kitchen for a cup of hot chocolate before they got their diaries and headed down to the castle. Just before they went, their mum spoke to them:

"I know you are all excited about the new puppies, but can you all keep them secret from the others for now? Dad and I want to talk something over and would rather people didn't know about them just yet."

The children were very curious about this, but promised their mum not to say anything.

"But Kayla knows," said Tess. "Shall I tell her not to say anything?"

"I don't think she is likely to talk to the castle family as they are all at senior school, or to Tyler either. She doesn't live near them. Don't worry about it, Tess. It's just for a few days while we think about a good idea dad had."

As it was such a lovely day, the children were allowed to ride their bikes down to the castle. Tess was thrilled. It was the first proper outing on her new bike. She was so proud of it! They rode down the narrow lane from the farm to the main road to Dorchester, then down to the village of Lesser Syding. At the entrance to the castle were two stone pillars with lions on the top of them. Once there had been fine gates, but now they were no longer there. The drive to the castle was straight and lined with fine beech trees on each side.

When they arrived they found that Tyler was already there. Tyler was Theo's best friend, and everyone called them the 'Two T's'. A few weeks previously, Tyler's little sister Sunshine, who was only two and a half, had been accidentally injured by a poacher shooting a pheasant. It had been a very nasty injury, but now she was doing well, and the culprits were safely behind bars, for they had run away from the scene of the accident and not got help for the little girl.

"Hi, Ty!" said Paul. "How is Sunshine today?"

"She's fine. I left her playing with her little kitten over in Gran's vardo," answered Tyler. Tyler and his parents along with Sunshine lived in Honeysuckle Cottage at the edge of the woods. His dad was a forester and managed the woods for the Forestry Commission. They were Romany gypsies but no longer travelled around. His grandmother lived at the back of the cottage in her painted wagon, called in the Romany language a 'vardo'. Her pony called Sparks was now kept in the castle stables where Felicity, who was usually called Flick, took care of him, although all the children rode him from time to time.

"I think we should start the meeting," said Seb (short for Sebastian), who was Flick's twin brother.

Everyone sat around the kitchen table. It was warm there with the range burning.

"Let's start with our nature diaries. Has anyone got anything special to share?"

"I have!" Tim piped up at once, looking excited. "I have seen a kingfisher in the trees by the river at the back of the farm. It was amazing, such a bright blue and much smaller than I thought it would be. It kept darting into the water and then back to the tree. I stayed and watched it for ages."

"Wow!" said Theo. "You lucky thing. I keep hoping to see one and never do. I did see some dippers, though, in the river here in the castle grounds. I'd never seen them before and had to look in the bird book to find out what they were."

No one else had seen anything really unusual, but it had been a difficult month what with Sunshine being hurt and then the weather being foggy and miserable.

"We've got something else to talk about, though," said Seb. "Mum has had a letter from Oxford. So long as we don't get any more snow, then the archaeological team is to come and start excavating the Roman site on Monday. They will mostly go home at the weekend, which is a shame, but as the evenings get a bit lighter, we can go and see what they are doing and what they have found. The team will have three professors and three students. They'll stay as guests here, and mum is even going to cook in the evenings for them to make it easier. She has decided too that the swimming pool can be back in action. We are going to clean it this afternoon, and then she will fill it again."

"That's really good news!" said Paul. "Can we come and have a swim sometimes?"

"Of course you can. All the gang are welcome, you should know that! Mum said she will let the vicar know too so that the youth group can put swimming onto their programme again as well as coming here to play snooker or table tennis," answered Seb.

"Mum had another idea too," Flick announced. "This year is very unusual because Valentine's Day and Pancake Day are in the same week and in half-term too. She thought we could have a pancake party. We would have to do the planning and help Mum. Penny will be home from school. We don't have long to plan it, but what do you think?"

"Wouldn't that be fun!" exclaimed Tess. "I'll help, and I bet Mum would too!"

"My mum and gran will help too, I'm sure," said Tyler. "Who would we ask? We need to decide today and make invitations to take to school on Monday. Also, we need to think exactly what to do to make it fun."

The children put their heads together and came up with all sorts of ideas, some good and others, well, not really possible! They made a list of people. As well as their families, they thought they should invite the archaeologists and students (though they might not want to come), the church youth group and Sid and Edie, who lived in Lesser Syding. Sid helped to do the castle garden. Then Theo came up with a suggestion.

"Perhaps we could each invite one person from our class at school who doesn't go to church or anything like that, so that we could show them that Christians have fun?"

They thought about it and decided it was a good idea. Sally, Theo and the twins' mum, came into the kitchen, and they shared their plans with her. They worked out roughly how many people might come and how many pancakes they would have to make! They planned some inside activities and even some outdoor ones should the weather be reasonable.

"It's lunchtime. How about I ring your parents and see if you can all have lunch here and then you can make invitations?" Theo's mum suggested.

When Sally talked to the other parents, they were very happy not only to let the children spend the afternoon planning, but also to help out.

"Don't worry about the eggs or milk," said Mrs Jenkins. "We have plenty to spare. When you have decided on other food, let me know and I'll get baking!" she added.

Tyler's mum and gran were equally enthusiastic. "We'll help. You have enough to do with your guests needing dinners as well as bed and breakfast!" said Betty, Tyler's mum. "I promised Sunshine that she could make heart-shaped cookies for Valentine's Day. They may not be perfect, being made by a two year old, but she would love to be part of the fun."

With only a week and a half to go before the party, everyone had to work very hard to get ready. Tess had already decided to ask Kayla, but then remembered the puppies. Maybe she should ask her mum first, in case Kayla 'let the cat out of the bag.' Then Tess giggled to herself—it wasn't the cat, it was the dog!

Paul, on the other hand, was struggling. He thought perhaps he should ask Cane. Cane and his family had come to live in the cottage next to Sid and Edie just before Christmas, but they had caused so much trouble to everybody. It was Cane's father and older brother who had been poaching and caused Sunshine's accident. Yet since then, Cane had really tried to 'turn over a new leaf,' and Paul had been playing football with him. He knew that it was right to forgive your enemies, but how would the rest of the gang feel if Cane came to the party, especially how would Tyler's family feel? In the end, he decided he would pray about the problem and then talk to his dad before he made up his mind.

Chapter Three

The archaeologists arrived and took up residence at the castle. They had a caravan which they parked near the site of the 'dig'. It contained most of the equipment they needed. The experts were two men and a lady, and there were two boys and one girl student. When Theo arrived home from school with Tyler, who usually came to do homework with him, they were introduced. The 'Two T's' thought they looked friendly and would be fun to have around, especially Chris, Pip and Daisy who were the students.

After the boys had finished their homework, Tyler was collected by his father and Theo went out to look after his hens. At Christmas he had been devastated when a fox had got into his henhouse and killed them all. Now he had some new ones from a rescue centre, and they were settling down and beginning to lay well. His chicken coop had been reinforced, and he felt it was now safe. As he wandered through the outhouses, Chris and Pip followed him. He secured all the chickens and told them about the fox and how he had rescued these hens. Then Theo went to find the ducks and shut them in the barn, and the students met the ducks and also Sparks the pony. They asked Theo to show them around, and he was glad to do so.

"Mum is heating the swimming pool now that you are here," Theo told them eagerly. "I am pleased as I am in the school squad and now I can practice again every day. Do you guys swim?"

"Yes, I do, "answered Chris, "but nobody told me to bring swimming trunks, so I'll have to make a trip to Dorchester to get some."

"I love swimming and did bring my trunks," said Pip, "but I thought I might have to go to the beach at Weymouth!"

"Wow! That's too cold by far!" answered Theo. "I usually swim after I have seen to the hens and before we have supper. There is even a shower in the changing room. We have a snooker table and table tennis in one of the old stables too."

"Wow! I am a 'townie' myself and thought it would be boring staying in the country all week, but it looks as if I might be wrong!" Pip told Theo.

"Next week is half-term, and we are having a party on Tuesday, a pancake and Valentine celebration. You will be welcome to join in if you want to!" commented Theo.

"We'll think about it," Chris answered. "I'm going to read up about Roman Dorchester before supper, so I'll leave you to have your swim. What about you, Pip?"

"I'll join Theo, if that's alright," he replied.

Theo loved having someone to swim against. Pip was really good and put him through his paces, and Pip was impressed with Theo's ability. After a little while, Seb and Flick arrived back from homework club at school and joined in the fun.

Then the children all helped their mother serve the guests their evening meal before having their own. Everyone was talking about the Roman remains. The professors felt that the castle site could be very important. It seemed to cover a large area. They would know more after the geophysics was done. Seb asked what that was, and one of the professors explained that it was a sort of scan of the area and would reveal the key areas of the site so that they would know where to dig. It was a sort of way to make a map of what was hidden underground.

It all sounded very complicated but interesting too. Theo had always loved history and just loved living in a castle. He knew that parts of it were quite old, dating to Tudor times. Now they would find out about when the Romans lived on their grounds.

"I have a metal detector," Theo told the guests. "Tyler and I found some silver spoons and a pirate's pistol using it!"

"You may find Roman coins in the grounds, but while the dig is going on we will have to ask you not to use it. But you can always come and help us dig!"

"Can I really?" asked Theo, his eyes shining. That would be something, to take part in a 'real dig'.

Theo was very glad it was half-term the following week and he could go out with the guests and help. It looked like it would be an exciting week, with the dig in progress and the party. Penny was coming home too; he was looking forward to seeing his big sister again.

Penelope was just sixteen and went to boarding school in Manchester. She had won a scholarship because she was so talented with music. Her main instrument was the piano, and one day she hoped she would be good enough to be a concert pianist. All her family were very proud of her.

The archaeological team settled in very well. Although cold, the weather was dry and they soon began to dig trenches and excavate the area. The geophysics scan had revealed a large area which looked like a villa and then something very interesting that the team thought might have been a kiln and also, something unexpected, there seemed to be a burial site. They began to scrape away at the area in a painstaking manner. Every little fragment of pottery or other household items were carefully put into polythene bags and labelled ready to go back to Oxford for investigation. As Chris explained to the children, although the whole project was exciting, the day to day mundane work of the dig could be quite boring.

Theo belonged to the history club at school, and when they met he told everyone about the Roman excavations in the castle grounds. The teacher who organized the club was very interested, and so Theo asked his mum if she could come home one evening for dinner so that she could meet the team. It was arranged that she would come one day in the half-term and see the site as well as get to know the team. The professors were enthusiastic and agreed to speak to the students of the history club and give them a conducted tour of the site at an appropriate time.

Chapter Four

On Friday afternoon when the children came home from school, the castle seemed very quiet because all the guests had gone home for the weekend. However, the next week was holiday, and there was so much to do. Most of the party plans were in place, and the invitations had been sent out. Flick had been helping her mum plan the food, because with the team staying there was a lot of extra work. Flick liked cooking; she even wondered if she might go to college and learn more about it after she'd finished school.

The phone rang, and it was Penny saying when her train was due to arrive in Dorchester. Theo and the twins all wanted to go to the station with their mum to collect her, so they ran to get their coats.

It was so good to be together again as a family! Of course, they didn't have their dad, because he now lived in Australia with his new wife and little girl, Lucy Jane. It still made them sad, but they had accepted the way things were and had learnt to forgive their father for leaving them.

Over supper that evening they told Penny all the news about the archaeologists who were excavating the site in the grounds and the plans for Tuesday's party. She was glad to be home!

The next morning, Penny saddled up Sparks and rode over to Tyler's home. She wanted to see his mum and gran because they had helped her in the Christmas holidays when she had been worried about things which were going on in her dorm at school. She also wanted to see Sunshine, whom she loved dearly and treated like a little sister.

Sparks cantered through the castle grounds and then trotted sedately down the road from Lesser Syding to Much Syding. Penny decided to take the short cut through the woods to Honeysuckle Cottage. As she rode along the path, she remembered how Sunshine had been hurt and left bleeding. How much she had prayed that God would make her better and how many times she had said 'thank you' when she had recovered. Penny had decided at that time that she wanted to become a real Christian and have Jesus in charge of her life, guiding and helping her and had asked him to come into her heart as her Lord and Saviour. She knew that he had answered her prayer, and her life was changed. Even so, it had been difficult through this past half-term in some ways. Her dorm mates had not understood and had teased her a lot when she began to read her Bible each day.

Now, they had accepted the fact that she didn't want to play the fortune telling games they so often played before 'lights out'. She read her Bible instead. Some of her friends were having terrible nightmares, and she was sure it was because of the games they played. When she woke in the night to hear them screaming or crying, she silently prayed for them. It had been hard, but God had really helped her to be bold. She found great joy in her music, and it always cheered her up to play the piano or the flute or to sing in the choir. Sometimes she wondered why God had given her such a gift. She loved her music but knew too that it would mean working very hard to develop the gift. Every day meant hours of practice as well as all the other school work to get good GCSE passes.

Sunshine heard the pony's hooves as Penny came near the cottage and ran out calling, "Sparkie!" Then she saw Penny and her little face beamed from one end to the other.

"Pen-Pen!" she shouted, loud enough to bring Gran out of her vardo. Penny dismounted and gathered the little girl up into her arms and hugged her. How good to see her none the worse following the accident.

Betty, Tyler and Sunshine's mother, came out of the cottage and hugged her visitor.

"Come on in, I'll put the kettle on," she said. Gran came over and they all sat around the kitchen table catching up with Penny's news. They had been praying for her because they knew it would not be easy to stand as a Christian when she returned to school.

Sunshine wanted to tell her all about the party. "Mummy and me will bake cookies" she lisped.

"We are baking on Monday morning, not today," her mum told her.

"Can I come and help?" asked Penny.

"Please, please Pen-Pen," begged Sunshine. "She can, can't she, Mummy?"

"Of course, that would be lovely, if your mum can spare you."

"I think she will. Flick loves to cook and has planned to take over our kitchen. I'll help Mum with breakfasts and then I'll come over. It sounds like a lot of fun is planned," Penny added.

Over at the Jenkins' farm, Paul had finished helping his dad with the pigs. "Now is a good time," he thought. All the week he had tried to get Dad alone to ask him about Cane. The party would soon be here, and he hadn't yet invited a friend to come.

"Dad, can you spare a minute to talk?" Paul asked. His father smiled. "Of course, Son. Come into the milking parlour and tell me what is on your mind."

As they walked over, Paul explained about wanting to invite Cane but not wanting to hurt his friends.

His father was silent for a minute or two.

"I think it would be alright. Cane wasn't actually involved in the accident, and although he was influenced by his brother and he bullied Flick, he has behaved at school ever since, hasn't he?"

"Yes, Dad, and he's not as stupid as people thought either, now that Jake doesn't stop him trying to learn. He stays for homework club and is catching up. I keep getting the words of Jesus come into my mind about loving those who are our enemies."

"I know that Bill has forgiven Cane's father and even visits him in prison," answered Mr Jenkins, "but I would like to give him a quick call to make sure they all feel comfortable about it."

"Thanks, Dad," said Paul and went back out into the farmyard. He saw Pickle with her puppies and laughed at their antics. Even little Omega had grown in the last week!

When his dad came out to him, he said it was fine to go and invite Cane and suggested why not ask his mother and younger brother and sister to come too?

Paul got out his bike and rode down the lane to Lesser Syding. He came to the row of cottages and parked his bike by Sid and Edie's fence. He then went to the next door and knocked. There was no answer. He peered in the window, but no one was around and although there was furniture, it all somehow had a deserted look. Paul thought it was strange. Cane had been at school all last week. Maybe they had gone back to London for half-term, though he thought Cane would have talked about it because he had loved London so much and hated living in the country.

Paul decided to knock at Sid and Edie's door. Maybe they would know. Edie had tried so hard to befriend the family, especially after the father and Jake had been sent to the prison and young offenders' institute after the poaching incident.

Edie opened the door, delighted to see her young friend.

"Come in, Paul. Nice to see you!"

"I came to see Cane and invite him to the Pancake party on Tuesday, but no one seems to be at home. I thought you might know if they have gone away for half-term," he explained.

"Sid and I are not really sure," she answered. "After school yesterday a white van came and everyone piled into it. They not only had suitcases as if going on holiday but all sorts of other personal belongings too. We wonder if they have just taken off and left, without saying goodbye to anyone. I am sorry if that is what they have done, just as we were beginning to make friends. I feel really sorry for that mother; she has had a hard time!"

"Well, I shall know after the holiday, I guess. It seems as if Cane won't be here for the party anyway. How about you and Sid—I hope you're coming?"

"Of course, we wouldn't miss it! We had such a good time at Christmas when we came to the Wildlife Society pantomime!" answered Edie. "It's so good of you children to include us 'oldies'. Can't tell you how much that means!

Anyway, I promised to go up to the castle and lend a hand getting it all ready. I'm good at tossing pancakes!"

Paul rode home thoughtfully, wondering what had happened to Cane and his family. He sent up a little prayer asking God to bless them all. The children had all experienced a pretty unhappy childhood from what he had gathered.

Tess had also talked to her mum about Kayla. "I really want to ask her to the party, Mum," she said. "She would love it, 'cos she has no one to play with and it's always so quiet in her house. But—" and Tess hesitated.

"But what?" asked her mum.

"It's about the puppies. Kayla is the only one who knows about Pickles' babies, and you told us not to breathe a word to anyone else. She might mention it to the others."

"You go on and ask her. If you like, you can ask her to a 'sleepover' here afterwards and tell her parents I will collect her and also take her home the next day. If she happens to talk about the pups, well, don't worry too much. I was just trying to keep a secret and make a surprise. When they are old enough to leave Pickles, I want to give one to Tyler and another to Theo, but I must talk to their parents first. Dogs cost a lot to keep with food, vet fees and things like that. I don't want the boys to know we have puppies and perhaps ask about having one before I have sorted things out. They also need proper training, and since there is no 'puppy school' near here, it will mean the boys having to do it themselves. That takes time, but the dogs must be trained not to worry the sheep or run after the chickens, ducks or wildlife. I'll talk to their folks at the party if I get time, but for now don't say anything but also don't worry if Kayla does."

"Oh, Mum!" Tess said in excitement. "The 'Two T's' will be so excited if they have puppies. I am sure they will both look after them well; they both love animals. The puppies can learn to be guard dogs for the hens and for Sunshine too, in case she ever wanders off into the woods again!"

"That was partly what was in my mind and why I haven't advertised them all for sale. Also, although Kayla can't have a pet at home, I thought you and she could share Omega, since he will need special care and training and of course, was born on your birthday!"

"Oh, Mum, thank you poooooo much!" said Tessa, giving her mum a hug. "Can I go and phone Kayla and ask her to the party and sleepover?"

"I'll come with you and then I can talk to her mother as well. Don't tell her about Omega yet. We'll keep that a secret until the puppies are big enough to leave their mum."

Chapter Five

On the Monday of half-term, the team of archaeologists returned. The children at the castle were pleased to see them, but everyone was far too busy preparing for the party to be able to go and see what they were doing or help with the dig.

It was a bright, sunny day, and that in itself helped everyone to feel cheerful. Penny, once she had done her piano practice, saddled up Sparks and rode to Honeysuckle Cottage to keep her promise and help Sunshine make heart-shaped cookies. The two girls worked together, and with Penny's help Sunshine did very well. Meanwhile, in the vardo, Gran was helping Tyler to make up a quiz, mostly about wildlife since the party was the idea of the Wildlife Society. Gran had never been to school so was unable to read or write, but she had so much knowledge about the environment, it was amazing! Once the quiz was finished, Tyler's dad allowed him to use the computer and printer to make copies. Tyler planned it to be a team quiz to make it more fun for everyone.

Flick and her mum were cooking pizzas and quiches. Even Seb was helping by scrubbing potatoes because they thought it would be nice to have jacket potatoes as a February evening could be very cold! Theo had been sent on a mission to several of their friends around the village to borrow frying pans, not only to be used for cooking pancakes, but also to have a pancake race if the weather was fine.

There was a lot of activity up at the farm too. Mrs Jenkins was the best cake maker in the village, and Tess was helping her make lots of cupcakes with red icing for Valentine's Day. Tess had also cut out lots of red paper hearts and made them into streamers as a decoration. Tim had gone out to the village shop to buy lemons, enjoying the bike ride in the sunshine. As usual he looked at every car parked by the road and noticed everyone which drove through the village. He passed the milk tanker on its way to collect the milk from their farm, and he waved to the driver. In the village shop, one of his classmates was buying some sweets. They stopped and chatted, and Tim asked him to the party as up until then he still hadn't invited a guest. The boy grinned and said he'd come if his mum would let him and asked what time it ended so that he could be collected for taking home.

Paul, once he had finished helping his dad with the pigs, began to work out a treasure hunt around the castle and its grounds. It was great fun to make up clues. His dad had advised him to have clues that were in the outbuildings or very near the castle so that the guests wouldn't be wandering all over the grounds in the dark.

"We don't want anyone falling into the lake or getting into the excavations," he said. "Why don't you make it so that people do it in twos, maybe an adult with a child? That way everyone should be safe."

"Good idea, Dad. I've got lots of good clues. What can we have as the prize?" asked Paul.

They put their heads together and thought for a while.

"Maybe it should be fairly simple. What about a box of chocolates for the adult and a box of sweets for the child?" suggested Mr Jenkins. "I'll give you some money and you can go to buy them."

"Thanks, Dad, that's a good idea," responded Paul.

Later in the day, the children met together at the castle and were very excited because everything seemed to be going so well. They were having fun preparing for the party and hoped everyone who came would also have fun. They arranged to meet the next morning and decorate the barn as well as the castle's main lounge, as both venues would probably be used.

How glad they were that it was a fine day for the party! It began early since it was winter, and most people arrived about five thirty, just as the sun was setting. All the Christmas outdoor lights had been fitted up, thanks to the three students staying at the castle, so it was light enough to have the pancake race and do the treasure hunt. Chris, Pip and Daisy were really good sports and wanted to join in. The three professors stayed in the kitchen chatting to the adults who felt they were too old to run down a field with a frying pan or take part in a treasure hunt. They were helpful making sure everyone had a drink as needed and things like that.

The pancake race was a great success. All those who took part had to run around a track which Sid had marked out in the grounds. Halfway round he had marked a spot where the contestants had to toss the pancake and catch it again before they could continue the race back to the barn. It was hilarious! The pancakes went everywhere! Everyone was so surprised because the winner turned out to be Kayla, and they all gave her a huge clap. She was glad it was dark and no one could see her blush! Although she was not terribly good at running, she had a steady hand and tossed her pancake, catching it at the first attempt. Her prize was a lovely china mug covered in small red hearts with "I love you" written on it and full of chocolate hearts! She thought it was one of the nicest things she had ever had and was so happy because she had never won a race before!

The treasure hunt came next. Paul had really organised it well and had made up very clever clues that set everyone thinking. It had been a brilliant idea to have teams of an adult with a child. Almost everyone wanted to join in, and there was a great buzz of activity. Pip was doing the hunt with the friend whom Tim had asked to come, and when they were looking for a clue about the outside of the castle wall, he became very interested in something else he found. Being a history student, he noticed one area of stones which didn't quite match the rest and on looking closer was sure it was a blocked up doorway. There wasn't time to examine it then, but Pip made a mental note to come back and have a better look in the daylight. "Who knows what might lie behind that?" he thought to himself. He had been so distracted that although he had been doing well in the treasure hunt, now he had fallen behind.

In the end it was the female professor who won with her partner, who was a girl from the church youth group. They worked out the last clue just seconds before the vicar and his young son! Both were delighted with their prizes.

By the time it was over, everyone was ready to eat. All the food had been taken to the barn. The highlight was the pancakes! They were being cooked in the kitchen and ferried over to the barn, but fortunately they were still hot and gorgeous! With all the fun outside. it was amazing how much everyone ate! Afterwards, as they were sipping hot drinks, the vicar told them how Pancake Day, or Shrove Tuesday as it really is called, came about. He also told everyone about the real Saint Valentine and emphasized how much we all need to love and be loved, but most of all, come to know how much God loves each of us and learn what he did to show it.

Next came the quiz which Tyler had prepared. He explained to everyone about the Wildlife Society and how they kept nature diaries. He told them about the exciting plans they had for the future, that one day the castle would have a wildlife centre which other people could visit and enjoy. Then they organised teams and had a go at the quiz. The children in the wildlife society were not allowed to take part, so they helped clear up some of the dishes. The winning team were all presented with pencils and notebooks so that they could start their own nature diaries. (That had been Gran's idea!)

To round off the party, Tyler's mum and dad produced their violin and guitar and played some folk music, ending with a couple of country dances. Even Penny and Sunshine danced together. Penny marvelled at the way Sunshine danced, even as a two year old! It seemed that Romany Gypsies were born with dancing feet!

When it was time for everyone to go home, it was evident that people had enjoyed themselves very much. Pip was heard to say as they were clearing up, "To think that I thought being in the country would be dull!" Paul laughed when he heard that, but it did make him sad to think that Cane and his family had missed out and had not been able to see that living in the country could be great fun.

Chapter Six

Kayla was so excited! It was the first time she had been asked to have a 'sleepover' since she had moved to Dorset. She knew that her father had moved to the country so that he could pursue his important work for the government, but it was very hard to be so far away from her grandparents, uncles, aunts and cousins as well as former school friends. She knew too, that her daddy's work was secret and that he could not talk about it, even to her. He was always kind and loving to her but seemed to live in his own world, and she only saw him at breakfast and supper time. When they had lived in London, Kayla had had a nanny because her mummy was also out at work for long hours. She knew that now she was nine she was really too old for a nanny, but Nanny Sue had been great fun and done all sorts of fun things with her. She really missed her now but was so glad that she had made friends at school with Tessa. Tess was the best artist in the class and although she found other work really hard, she wasn't stupid as some people called her. One day Kayla had talked to her mother about this, and her mother had told her that some of the world's greatest brains like Einstein and Sir Winston Churchill had been 'slow learners' to start with. She also told

Kayla to stick up for her friend and always help her, and she really tried to do that.

After the party all the children were tired and ready to go to bed. It had been huge fun, but it was long past all their bedtimes! Before they went to their rooms, Mr Jenkins gathered the children around him and said a prayer, thanking God for the wonderful day and for keeping everyone safe and asking Him to give everyone a good night's rest. They all said 'Amen' before they went upstairs. This was something new to Kayla. She didn't know if her parents ever prayed, but certainly not out loud or with her.

Tess had a lovely room under the eaves of the house, which meant the roof sloped down. It was not very big, but there had been room to make up a small bed for Kayla. Almost as soon as their heads touched their pillows, they fell asleep. Mrs Jenkins let the girls 'lie in' in the morning. When they did wake, they smelt the wonderful smell of bacon wafting up the stairs.

"Mummy must be cooking breakfast," Tess said to Kayla. "Let's go down in our PJ's and have some!"

Mr Jenkins came for his breakfast when the morning milking was finished and ate with the family.

"When you are showered and dressed, if you like, you girls can come and help me with the lambs," he suggested. They needed no second bidding! As quickly as they could, they got ready to go to the barn and bottle-feed the lambs. They found Mr Jenkins cuddling a very scruffy little lamb.

"Look at this little mite!" he said. "I heard a mother ewe making a great noise in the upper pasture, so I went to see what the trouble was. She had lost her lamb, this little one. I couldn't see him anywhere, so I tramped around the pastures to look for him. Eventually, I heard a pitiful wail, and the little fellow had got himself into a ditch in the far side of the next field! He was caught in brambles and unable to get free. When I picked him up, he was so cold and shivering that I thought I should bring him down into the barn for the time being, just to watch he is ok. Will you hold him and keep him warm and safe for me while I go up and collect his mum and her other lamb and bring them down here?"

Mr Jenkins handed the lamb to Kayla, and she felt very honoured to cuddle him. "Shall we give him a bottle, too?" Tess asked her dad.

"Good idea, love," he answered, so Tessa went off to get one while Kayla wrapped the lamb in a blanket and cuddled him.

The lamb gulped down the milk; he must have been away from his mother for quite a long time.

"It's just like the story of the lost sheep!" remarked Tessa.

"What story is that?" asked Kayla, who loved reading and loved stories.

"It's a Bible story. We were told about it recently at the after-school Bible club, but I have heard it in Sunday school too. Once there was a shepherd and he had a hundred sheep in his flock. They didn't stay out in the pasture all the time like our sheep do, probably because there were wolves and lions and animals like that who would prey on them. Each night the shepherd collected his sheep and put them into a pen, then lay down over the doorway making himself like a gate. If a wild beast or even a sheep rustler came, he would immediately drive them away. Then in the morning he would lead his sheep to really good pasture for the day.

"One night, this shepherd was counting his sheep into the pen, and he only counted ninety-nine. One had gone missing! Even though he was tired, he left the other sheep safely in the pen and went searching everywhere until he found the lost sheep. When he had found it, he put it on his shoulder and brought it back to the pen. The shepherd was so happy that he called his friends to have a party because he had found his lost sheep.

"The point of the story is that Jesus is like that Good Shepherd and knows every one of us. He knows when we have run away or wandered down a path and got lost and comes looking for us. He comes to find us and carry us back home."

"That's a really cool story," commented Kayla. "I have never heard about it, but Mum and Dad don't go to church. I wonder if there is a Bible at home. I'll have a look. We have hundreds of books, so there must be one somewhere."

The rest of the day whizzed past, and before she knew it, Kayla had to get ready to go home.

"It's been fantastic. Thank you so much for inviting me," she said to Mrs Jenkins.

"We have loved having you, and you must come again soon," Tess's mum replied, and the girls looked at each other and grinned in delight.

Chapter Seven

Theo was up early the morning after the party. He wanted to go to the site and help Chris, Pip and Daisy with the excavations. Tyler was cycling over to join them, and Seb said he and Flick would also come and help. It was amazing to be able to help uncover real history! Once he had finished looking after the chickens and ducks, Theo was free to go up to the site. He put on his wellies and his oldest anorak and went to join the archaeologists. Chris showed him how to use a trowel and gently scrape away the layers of soil and what to look for. After about half an hour, Tyler arrived, followed quickly by Seb and Flick. They worked hard all morning, and all found fragments of pottery and some coins. Seb found what appeared to be a gold necklace, which excited them all. Before they all had a lunch break, the items were put into bags and labelled and stored in the caravan.

They ate their packed lunches together in the caravan, and the children felt very grown up, especially when the lady professor began to tell them about Roman Dorchester. She told them how the area had been inhabited for many years, for there were Stone Age and Iron Age remains. The Romans had arrived in AD 43 and quickly invaded the Dorset area. A town, but mostly of wooden buildings, called

Durnovaria was built about AD 60. Later on in the second century AD, stone buildings were erected and the town was fortified with a ditch. The town had a forum and a market place lined with shops and public buildings, including baths. The water was brought into the town by an aqueduct.

There were some beautiful villas where rich people lived, and these were heated by a form of central heating. These expensive villas even had mosaic floors. The lady explained that there was a good example of a Roman villa in Dorchester which they could go and visit and also that a little of the stone wall which was added much later to enclose the town was still visible.

The children were surprised to learn this, for although they only lived a few miles away from the town, they had never visited these places. They decided to put it on their 'must do' list.

The afternoon was even better! As they scraped away, layer by layer, they found bits of a mosaic floor! It was so amazing to think that they were discovering a picture made of little coloured tiles that had been hidden for centuries! It was painstaking work as slowly each little section was uncovered. Nothing must be damaged! Chris explained to the children that the site was going to be very important. It could be even as important as the Roman villa in Dorchester. The scan had showed that the site covered quite a large area, and it looked like the outline of a villa as well as other buildings and the possible burial site.

"We shall probably be here for quite a few weeks, then we'll have to go back to Oxford and return at a later date, if your mother allows us to do so," Daisy told them. "I hope I am allowed to stay on the team, but I do have exams to work for as well. I might be able to spend some of the summer vacation here."

"I'm sure Mum won't mind, but she may have other visitors booked in during the summer. Some of our guests like to come back regularly," remarked Theo.

When the afternoon work was finished, Pip said to Theo that he would like to have another look at the castle because he was intrigued by what he had seen the previous evening when they were doing the treasure hunt. It looked like a blocked off door at basement level.

"Do you have a basement or cellars?" he asked Theo.

"Oh, yes," Theo replied. "There is quite a large cellar where wine used to be stored. Now it's full of junk. Do you want to go down there?"

"Please," answered Pip. "Can I explore it before we go and swim?"

"I'll take you as soon as we get home, while we still have our dirty clothes on, because it's pretty mucky down there!" Theo commented.

When they reached the kitchen, Theo found the large, old key to the cellar. He grabbed a torch, because there was only one small bulb to light the cellar, as he remembered. Nobody ever bothered to go down there, not since dad had gone to Australia. He had kept some of his wine down there when he lived at home.

The stairs were stone and much worn. Theo was glad he had the torch. It smelt very musty and dusty, and there were cobwebs everywhere. In fact, Theo was quite glad that Pip was with him because it was a bit spooky and sent shivers down his spine. It was cold too!

As Theo had warned Pip, there was a lot of junk there! It had old fashioned mangles and tin baths, bottles and stone jars and rusty bits of metal, all sorts of rubbish.

"Maybe we should have a clear out and take some of this stuff to the recycling centre and the dump," Theo thought to himself.

Pip was busy looking at the walls. He borrowed the torch and examined the stones very carefully.

"Look, Theo," he said as he pointed out stones which were slightly different in colour and shape to all the others on the walls. "This was once a doorway. Strange though, it is not on the outside wall like the blocked up doorway I saw outside. This cellar is very old, part of the original manor house, I think. I wonder what is behind? I think you may have a blocked-off room. I wonder what it is and why it was blocked off."

"I don't think we have any other room except the cellar under the house," said Theo. "I'll ask Mum if we can look at the plans. I am sure some of the old plans were given to us when we bought the castle. Mum knows a little of its history, but not that much. Shall we go and ask her?"

They went back upstairs, and Theo was glad to get back into the warmth and light of the kitchen. He asked his mum about the old plans of the castle, and she promised she would have a look for them. Meanwhile, Pip went again to the outside and examined the blocked-up doorway. He scraped a little of the mortar away and decided it had been blocked up a very long time ago. He always liked a mystery, which was partly how he came to study history. He loved to find out what had happened in the past!

Theo, too, loved mysteries. He kept wondering about the blocked-off room. He sent a text to Tyler about it, and they made up theories that perhaps someone had been murdered there and the room had been blocked off. Maybe there was still a body there? Or even a ghost? Their imaginations ran wild!

Sally found the old plans and maps of the castle. They were very dog-eared and fragile. After her guests had finished supper, she told Pip that he could look at them, and he spread them out on the dining room table. He poured over them for ages trying to work out where everything fitted in.

"Got it!" he shouted in delight. "Look! This must be the basement layout, and there is another room indicated."

Theo and his mum looked where Pip was pointing and sure enough, it did look as if there was another room under the castle.

"See, Mum, it has three doors," said Theo in excitement. "One to the outside, one into the cellar and one on the other side. Where would that be?"

"Let's work it out," said Pip. "We need the plans of the next floor." And he unrolled another sheet of very faint plans and studied them for a while.

"If I am right," he said, "the other door should be off the turret."

"But I sleep in the turret, and I am sure there is no blocked-off door at the bottom of the stairs!" remarked Theo.

"Theo, it's now plastered and painted. You probably wouldn't know if there was once a doorway there," said his mum. "Anyway, it's time you went to bed. You and Pip can look tomorrow. Even if you find a blocked-up door, I'll have to think hard as to whether I'm prepared to have the place knocked about! I don't want my house falling down around my ears! However, I agree it's interesting."

Pip looked at Theo and gave him a grin. "We'll explore tomorrow when I've finished work, shall we?"

"Yes, please," answered Theo and then said goodnight to everyone and climbed his hundred steps to bed. He did look carefully at the wall at the bottom of the stairs, but couldn't see anything strange.

Chapter Eight

The next day, the 'Two T's' decided to go again and help with the dig. The twins had gone to Dorchester with Penny to do some shopping and then see a film. Paul, Tim and Tessa were hoping to come down later in the day but were going out with their mother first.

As they worked, gradually more and more little pieces of the mosaic floor were being found and pieced together. The boys could now see how this could once have been a house. They were working with Pip and one of the professors. Chris and the other male professor were working nearby, discovering something very unexpected. They seemed to be unearthing a kiln where pottery was fired! The Romans introduced kilns to Britain around AD 43. These kilns had two chambers, the top one where pots were placed and underneath another chamber with a fire box. The roof was formed by placing broken pottery or turf on top of the chamber. The pottery was not protected very well from the flames or the ash from the burning wood in the fire chamber, and it was unglazed. Bill and the professor had found a heap of broken pottery which seemed to form a roof, underneath which was a chamber with some pots, and beneath that was a chamber which was blackened by fire. They were both very excited, never having seen a kiln like it before except in books. The lady professor took lots of photos. and she and Daisy went to help with the excavation. They did not want to dismantle all the structure but leave it to be a living museum if possible. Of course, the land belonged to Theo's mum, but already she had decided that the villa's remains should stand as a monument to the past and be open eventually for the public to visit. It didn't seem right to cover it all up again with earth and turn it back into a meadow. It wasn't as if she was a farmer and needed to graze the land.

At lunchtime, Pip and the 'Two T's' talked about the hidden room under the castle. At breakfast Theo's mum had talked to Pip and asked how invasive it would be to try to unblock the door. He felt that it could be done stone by stone without causing any problem because these old castles were so well built on good foundations, but he would get expert advice before he started.

When they had all finished working, Tyler stayed at the castle to go with Pip and Theo so they could investigate the turret stairs. They were all disappointed not to find any evidence of a door. They went back into the cellar, and Pip looked very carefully at the blocked-off door there, then outside and looked at that one. He felt the best way would be to try and unblock the cellar entrance. At least it would be dry inside should the weather change.

After they had all showered and changed, Pip went on the internet to talk to some of his friends and also his father, who was a builder, to get advice. He also told his parents that he wanted to stay at the castle that weekend so that he could begin on the doorway on Saturday.

Theo's mum had some other guests coming for the weekend, but Pip's room was still free and so he could stay on. The 'Two T's' were very excited when the weekend came, and they joined Pip down in the cellar. They had to wait until all the B&B guests had gone so that the noise would not disturb them. Pip's father had told him how and where to begin, and he carefully managed to dislodge a stone at the top of the doorway. The mortar was old and scraped away easily. The stone was very heavy, but the three of them managed to remove it.

They gasped when they peered inside the hole. Nothing had prepared them for what they saw! Theo in his excitement ran upstairs and called for his mother to come and see. Inside the hole, they could see a chapel or church of some kind!

Once the first stone was out, it was easier to remove the others. It almost took all the morning, but in the end they had uncovered the doorway and were able to go in. Once inside, they were able to find the door which once had led to the outside. What Pip had thought was a door to the turret stairs, was in fact, a window. It was hard to see with the built up wall behind it, but it looked like stained glass. In front of it stood a carved table on which was placed a wooden stand. Resting on the stand was a very big book. When they looked at it, they could see it was a New Testament, but the English seemed strange. There were some old carved chairs and kneelers. It looked as if woodworm had been feasting on them, and Pip warned them not to sit down in case they collapsed. The dust of years lay on all the furniture, and the boys began sneezing.

"Time to come up, clean up and have some lunch," announced Sally, Theo's mum. "It's amazing, a chapel of our own in the castle! We must try and find out more about it, but for now, food!"

Actually, the three boys were starving, and it was well past lunchtime. Once they had eaten, they were sent out to get some fresh air, so they walked up to the lake looking for wildlife. They took Pip to the river because he had never seen an otter, but today, much to his disappointment, the otters were not out playing. The 'Two T's' told Pip all about the plans for a wildlife sanctuary.

"I think you will have a living history experience too for people to visit," Pip commented, "not only the Roman site, but now a hidden chapel. I wonder why it was closed up and how old it is. We need to do some investigating!"

"I hope we can open it up again and make it a 'prayer space' like we have at school," said Theo.

"Whatever is a 'prayer space'?" asked Pip. The boys rather shyly explained about the little place at school where people could go and pray and pin up things they would like other people to pray about. Tyler told Pip how he had pinned up a request when his little sister, Sunshine, had been shot by accident and how God had answered their prayers.

Pip was thoughtful. "I haven't ever prayed, but it sounds a good idea. I know being with you all here at the castle and then at the party this week has made me think. You all seem to have something 'extra' in your lives which I don't understand."

"I think you will find it isn't 'something' but 'someone' extra, and He is Jesus. We have all been meeting Him in the past year or so, and He is the most wonderful friend," Theo tried to explain to this very clever student from Oxford University.

"You must tell me more another time!" Pip answered. "But now, I'd really like a swim before I log on to the computer and try to look things up!"

The boys ran back to the castle and got their trunks. They had a great time swimming and were still splashing around when the twins and Penny returned. They soon showered and dressed, ready to show them the new find in the castle!

Chapter Nine

It was hard to believe that half-term had come and gone so quickly! On Sunday morning the four children from the castle went to the village church. It was a bright morning, so they walked together to where the church was at Much Syding. It seemed as if the long, cold winter was at last evaporating into spring. The birds were singing, and even one or two violets had come out into flower. Some wild snowdrops gave a splash of white in the hedges, and some catkins were fully in bloom, looking lovely against the bright blue sky. The children were talking about the latest 'find' at the castle.

"I think Pip is going to look up on the internet about chapels in castles. It would make a fab 'prayer space' for our family and even the guests," said Theo.

"Did you look to see if there was a date in the New Testament?" questioned Penny. "That would give a clue about when it was last used."

"No," replied Theo, "it was so fragile that Pip said we shouldn't finger it."

"The furniture might also give some clues," said Flick.

"Your friend who is curator of Dorchester museum might be willing to come over and have a look. He was very helpful about that pistol you found," Seb suggested to Theo.

"That's a brill idea!" said Theo. "I think I still have his phone number in my mobile, and I could ring him after school tomorrow."

By the time they had reached the church, they were bursting with ideas. They shared them with Tyler and also with the Jenkins children after the "Live Wires" group had finished.

"Live Wires" had been interesting for Penny. They had a lively discussion about what pleased God and what made Him sad. Although she was quite shy and only was able to attend in the school holidays, she shared how hard it had been in her dorm not to take part in playing the game which she knew to be wrong. Theo felt very proud of his big sister that she had stood up for what was right. At the end of the session, she asked the group if they would pray for her while she was at school, that she would be strong and live like a Christian should. With all the music practices as well as working for her GCSE's, it was hard to find time to read her Bible before lights out. The leader offered to get some helpful reading notes for her and promised to drop them off at the castle that evening as Penny was leaving for Manchester on the early Monday morning train.

"Is there any time of the day when I can phone you and we can chat about things that are difficult, or I can email you if that is easier," the leader said.

"You can email me on my iphone," answered Penny. "Then I can always email or text you back. Thank you. It would be great to have a prayer buddy."

Penny went back to her school, and the others went back to the high school the next day. She always felt a bit homesick when she left the family, but once back with her friends it was alright. Now she felt really pleased that she had a 'prayer buddy'. She had music theory, singing and flute exams to take in the next half of the term, as well as a lot of assignment work for her GCSE's. She was very aware it would be tough. Even though she had won a scholarship to the music academy, it was still a sacrifice for her family to let her go. There were so many 'extras' to be paid for and then the fact that she wasn't at home to help in running the B&B like everyone else, so she felt she must work extra hard and make them all proud of her.

Tim and Tess went back to the village school. They were surprised that Cane's younger brother and little sister were not there. Maybe Paul was right when he thought they had taken themselves back to London again. At registration their names were called out, so the teachers must have expected them. At break, Tim went to Mr Stevens, the teacher for years six and seven, and told him that Paul thought the family had moved out.

It was the first day after half-term that Tim first noticed something. He was looking out of the window, trying to work out a sum, when a car pulled up. Tim knew just about every car in the village, and he was sure that he had not seen this one before. In fact, he had never seen one like it, only read about them in the magazine which his dad sometimes had and always let him share. It was a new design of Toyota and ran on both diesel and electric. It was supposed to be environmentally friendly and really economical too. He supposed he could almost include it in his wildlife diary, as it was 'green', if not wild!

"Tim, have you finished yet?" Mr Steven's voice brought him back to reality.

"Not quite, sir," he answered politely and began to work out the sum. When he looked out again, the car was no longer there. "Pity," he thought to himself. "I would like to have had a decko."

After school, when his mum had collected him and Tess, he kept his eyes peeled to see if he could spot the unusual car, but there was no sign of it. "I guess it was just a passing stranger stopping for a moment," he decided.

Tim did see the car again, though, the next day. Once again it was parked outside the school, just past the yellow zigzag lines outside the gates. It went before the school came out, which was very strange, because it meant it was not a parent collecting a child. Something about it puzzled Tim, though he couldn't think why. After all, the driver wasn't breaking the law, and people were at liberty to park on the side of the road so long as they were not on a yellow line!

On Thursday afternoon it was there again, and Tim saw there was a man in the driver's seat and a lady beside him. He noticed her because she wore a red duffle coat a bit like his mum's. As soon as class was finished, he forgot all about it because it was the after-school Bible club. He and Tess always stayed for this, and his mum collected them an hour later. He went to find Tess in her classroom who had just said goodbye to her best friend, Kayla, who had forgotten to ask her mum if she could stay. Tim liked Kayla too. She was alright, he thought, for a girl, even though others in the school thought her a swot. She was always kind to Tess and stuck up for her when she was teased about having to wear glasses or not being able to spell or do sums well. He grinned at her and said "Hi!" and she went just a bit pink and said "Hi" back.

Tim and Tess went into the hall and joined the group gathering there. They were going to play charades this afternoon and act out Bible stories. Tim had been practising at home and had fun looking up stories he could act. He hoped his team would win, because there were usually some sweets as prizes! Tim soon forgot about the car and also about Kayla, even though she had gone pink when he had greeted her!

Halfway through the club, when they had stopped for refreshments which Miss Roberts the infants' teacher had made, there was a commotion. The school caretaker came rushing in, telling Mr Stevens that there was a mum outside in tears. Mr Stevens asked Miss Roberts to look after the children while he went to sort things out. He had been a teacher for many years at the village school and knew all the families very well. He found the one mother he knew little about, Kayla's mother, very distraught. He sat her down in the office and asked her what her problem was. She was so upset it took a while for him to get the story. Apparently, she had been a little delayed leaving home to collect her daughter. This wasn't very unusual, and Kayla knew that if her mother wasn't at the gates then she could cross the road and go to the village stores to choose some sweets and wait for her mother there. The shopkeeper was quite happy with this arrangement because it was never for very long and only happened a couple of times a month. Today, when she realised she was a bit late, she drove to the shop. The shopkeeper had been surprised to see her because Kayla had not been in.

At first she wasn't too worried. Maybe Kayla was playing on the swings on the green or chatting to a friend. She hunted around everywhere, but there was no sign of her daughter, and no one had seen her. Much Syding was a small and friendly village, and everyone knew everyone else.

Mr Stevens looked worried as he listened to the story.

"I think, just to be on the safe side, we should call the police. We do have guidelines which we always follow with our children, so don't get alarmed or think the worst. There is probably some logical reason why she didn't go to the shop. Have you telephoned your husband in case she went home some other way?" he asked.

Kayla's mum did that, but her husband had no news. "Shall I come down to the school?" he asked.

"No, you stay there in case she gets home. Ring me if she does. Keep your mobile on. How I wish I had let her take one to school, but I thought she was too young!" Kayla's mum answered.

Knowing it might take the police a few minutes to come out from Dorchester, Mr Stevens made the poor mother a cup of tea and stayed with her while they waited. Silently, he prayed for Kayla, that wherever she was she would be safe. He prayed for wisdom for the police and strength for the parents. How glad he was that he could talk to his heavenly Father about everything that happened.

When the police came, he left them for a few moments to talk to Kayla's mother and went back to the Bible club. It was time for them to finish, but he knew that Kayla was Tess's special friend, so he felt he needed to talk to the children and pray with them, afterwards explaining that Kayla seemed to be lost but that the police were coming to help find her.

Chapter Ten

Tess was very upset by the news, and when her mother arrived to take her and Tim home, she just ran into her arms and sobbed. Before they left the school, the police asked Tess if Kayla had said anything to her about what she would do after school. Tess shook her head, too upset to answer.

"As soon as we get home we will look in the barns because Kayla loves to help feed the orphaned lambs and also see the new puppies we have," said Mrs Jenkins. "But she has never come to us uninvited, and it would be so unlike her to run off without telling her mother. We live quite a long way away too!"

Kayla's mother went to the police station and tried to help them by giving them a list of all Kayla's friends and her interests and describing in detail not just her school uniform but her winter jacket and outdoor shoes. The police needed a recent photograph of her and a piece of clothing for the police dogs to sniff and pick up her scent. A search was to be started at once, to cover as much of the local area as possible before dark.

By the time Tyler and Theo got off the school bus and went up to the castle, the news had spread throughout both villages. Nobody could believe that a child from Much

Syding School might have been abducted. Tyler decided he had better go straight home. He couldn't concentrate on homework anyway.

He borrowed Theo's bike and cycled home, taking the short cut through the woods. As he reached the cottage, he saw policemen, and felt a shiver going down his spine. It was too soon after Sunshine's accident, and the sight of the police brought it all back to him. Then he had another thought. What if the police were blaming his father? As gypsies, when they had first come to the village, they were blamed for everything! The local people seemed to think all gypsies were troublemakers, dirty and thieves! It had taken a long time to win the villagers' respect and confidence.

Tyler put Theo's bike away, locking it safe, for it was a very expensive one and not like his own, old boneshaker that no one would bother to steal! He went into the kitchen, and the local policeman was talking to his father. He turned when he saw Tyler come in and smiled.

"Hello, Tyler," he said. "We would like your dad to help us search the woods. He knows every inch of them, and we want to cover as much as we can as quickly as possible. A nine-year-old girl has gone missing from the village school," he explained.

"I know. I heard about it when I got off the school bus. It's Kayla, isn't it? I met her at the pancake party last week. A very quiet and clever girl and she's Tess's friend. Please, can I help with the search?"

"We need every bit of help we can get, but you must stay with your dad. You'll need a good stick to search the undergrowth for any little clue, like a hair ribbon or a tissue. Absolutely anything. Here is a whistle. If you find anything that you think might help, just blow it and don't touch the item. My officers will come and take it away."

Tyler had a quick drink, put on his wellies and old coat and joined his father combing every inch of the woods. There were six policemen and two dogs as well.

Almost every able-bodied person helped with the search, including the archaeologists. They searched their own properties, sheds and garages, gardens and the local footpaths. The farmers took their sheep dogs and searched the hills and fields. When it became dark, those who could continued with torches. The whole area echoed with the sound of people calling 'Kayla'. There was no trace of her at all.

The vicar phoned round all his parishioners and asked everyone who could to come to church that evening for an hour of prayer. The church was packed, and he led everyone in prayers for Kayla's safe return, for the police to know where to look and for Kayla's parents to be comforted.

Not many people had actually met Kayla's parents. The family had moved into the area just a few months before and lived in a big house a little way away from both villages. The house was very private and surrounded by a tall hedge. Although her mother drove her to and from school and shopped in the village, hardly anyone had met her father. The Jenkins family were the closest friends they had made. After the church prayer meeting, Mrs Jenkins took one of her special cakes up to their house, hoping to be able to comfort Kayla's mother, but the police were there and although they promised to give the cake to her, they were not able to let anyone visit as yet.

It seemed such a long night as the villagers waited, hoping to hear good news. None came. It was as if Kayla had vanished into thin air! The next morning, The Sydings seemed covered with a heavy cloud of worry and fear. Even the children who lived very close to the school who normally walked or cycled on their own were brought by their parents. Once the bell had gone, the teacher locked the school gate.

At assembly the head spoke to all the children about how they must never, ever talk to strangers. The local policeman, who was known to all of them, spoke to them as well and told them the same message.

He asked all the children to think. Had they seen any strangers in the village or anything unusual? He told them to come and see him afterwards if they could think of any little thing, because it might help them find Kayla.

"It might seem a silly thing to you. I don't mind. You will not be wasting my time, and it might help."

Then the headmaster prayed for Kayla and her parents before the children were dismissed to their classes.

With everything that had happened, Tim had totally forgotten the strange car until the policeman talked to them. "Why didn't I think about it before!" he thought to himself. "How stupid I am! Maybe someone in that car kidnapped Kayla!"

Tim ran from the hall to the school office. "I need to speak to the policeman," he blurted out. "I did see something strange and if only I had remembered yesterday it might have helped!"

The school secretary put her arm round him and led Tim into the headmaster's office where he was talking to the policeman.

"What is it, Tim?" asked both men when they saw him.

"Oh, sir," said Tim, now getting quite upset, "I was looking out of the classroom window at the beginning of the week and saw this unusual car. I noticed it because I had seen it in Dad's auto book but never seen a real one. It was dark blue, registration number EX 123 RIP and was a Toyota hybrid car. You know, one that runs on electric and diesel. It was there again when school ended on Wednesday and then again yesterday, and I would have liked to have taken a closer look at it, but I was not going home, but to

Bible club. Inside the car were a man and a lady. The man was in the driver's seat. The lady had a bright red coat and long golden hair. I know everyone's car in the village, because I love cars, but I have never seen this one before and I did not recognise the couple in it."

"That's so helpful, Tim," said the constable, looking almost cheerful. "Are you sure about the registration number?"

"Yes, sir," Tim replied. "Look, I wrote it in the corner of my exercise book. I know I shouldn't have, sir," he said, looking at the headmaster, "but it was such a strange one on such an interesting car."

"I think we'll forgive you on this occasion, Tim," said the head, smiling. "It's true, Constable, that Tim is renowned for knowing everyone's cars. He loves anything on wheels!"

Tim was sent back to his class. One or two other children came in and talked about finding an earring or a hairband, but nothing else significant. The constable alerted the C.I.D. officer who was now in charge of the case to hunt for the car and to get all the CCTV films from local areas examined to see if they could find the car in Dorchester or other nearby towns.

Somehow, with Tim's wonderful memory and accurate recording, everyone had new hope.

Chapter Eleven

After Kayla had said goodbye to Tess and Tim that fateful afternoon, she went out of the school gates, expecting to see her mum waiting for her. She nearly jumped out of her skin when a voice she recognised said, "Hello, sweetheart!" There getting out of a car by the gate was Nanny Sue! She hugged her in delight and wanted to ask her what she was doing in Much Syding, but her old nanny bundled her quickly into the back of the car, saying she would explain as they went along. The man driving the car started off almost before she had time to sit up and do up her seat belt.

"Did Mummy ask you to take me home?" asked Kayla. "I thought she was coming to meet me."

"Well, not exactly," replied Nanny Sue. "It's all to do with your daddy's work. We have to drive quite a long way, and you will stay with us for a while."

"But Mummy and Daddy didn't say anything, and I haven't packed anything. Can't I go home and get my things?" Kayla was feeling rather anxious. She sensed something was wrong. Somehow Nanny Sue looked troubled, and the man in the front kept turning round and frowning at them both. She sensed that her nanny wasn't telling her everything. Had her parents been hurt? Where was she going?

After they had been driving through country lanes for about an hour, she begged Nanny Sue to stop because she wanted the loo and felt a bit sick. When her nanny asked the driver, whom she called 'Jim', he swore and told them he would find a tree and she could go behind it.

"Why can't we find a proper toilet? I'm thirsty, too. Mummy always gives me a drink and biscuit after school. You know that, Nanny Sue."

"You'll do as you are told and shut up," growled Jim. Even Nanny Sue looked frightened of him.

When they eventually stopped, Kayla felt like running away, but it was in the middle of nowhere and Nanny Sue was nearby, watching her. As they went back to the car, her nanny told her in a whisper, "Don't be frightened, Kayla. I won't let any harm come to you."

As they climbed back into the car, Kayla wondered what Nanny Sue meant. Who would harm her? What was happening? Once again they drove off with speed. Kayla had no idea where they were. They seemed to be taking side roads, and she couldn't read the signposts because they were travelling so quickly. They almost collided with a tractor coming out of a farm gate, and Jim swore at the man driving it. Kayla thought he was a horrible man. Why was Nanny Sue with him? Nanny Sue held her hand and squeezed it from time to time, and that made her feel a little safer. Eventually, she felt drowsy and finally fell asleep.

It was dark when she woke up. The car had stopped outside a little stone cottage. It wasn't in a village, as far as she could see. There were tall fir trees all around the cottage, and there was an outhouse and an unkempt garden. Nanny Sue took her by the hand, and Jim opened the cottage door. It was cold inside. When he put the light on, she could see it was dirty and poorly furnished. Nanny Sue led her up the stairs to a small bedroom. There was a bed and a wardrobe in it, nothing else.

"This will be your room," her nanny told her. "Next door is where Jim and I will be sleeping. He is my husband. Then along the corridor is the bathroom. Most of the time you will have to stay in this room, Kayla," her nanny told her sadly. Kayla was about to protest when her nanny put her finger on her mouth and whispered, "Don't ask questions or make a fuss, sweetheart. I wish I could explain, but for the moment you have to just trust me that I will not let any harm come to you."

Jim had brought in a suitcase and plonked it in his and Nanny Sue's room. Then he brought in bags of provisions and dumped them on the kitchen table and told Nanny Sue to make some food for them all. "Can Kayla come and help me?" she asked Jim.

"No. I told you. She has to stay in the room away from us. If she doesn't do what she is told then I will tie her up. I don't want her running away. It won't take long before the police will be hunting up and down the land for her!" answered Jim. Nanny Sue looked frightened. "You promised me you would not hurt the child. I'll never forgive you if you lay a finger on her!"

Upstairs in the bedroom, Kayla could hear them arguing, but could not hear all that was said. She felt very frightened and alone. "How could Nanny Sue have married such a horrible man?" she thought. By now she realised that something terrible had happened and she had been taken away from her parents. She had been kidnapped! If only her mum had allowed her to take her mobile phone to school, then she could have phoned home and her parents would have come and rescued her!

The cottage was very cold, and Kayla shivered even though she was still wearing her outdoor coat. She sat on the bed and tried to work out how she could escape. Maybe in the morning she could try to open the window and climb out. At least she had her backpack with her school books. She could do her homework and read her book. Her tummy rumbled, and she wondered when she would have some food.

When Nanny Sue came up to see her, she was trying to do her school work sitting on the bed. It wrenched at her nanny's heart to see Kayla's tear-stained face.

"Good girl! You always did your homework well! Thank you for being quiet and staying up here. See, I have brought you some supper. It's spaghetti bolognaise. It used to be your favourite. I hope you still like it," she said.

"I do, Nanny Sue, and I am so very hungry now. Thank you," and Kayla tried to smile at her old nanny. She couldn't believe her nanny had let something bad like this happen to her.

"Am I a prisoner here?" she asked her.

"Well, sort of," replied her nanny. "You have to be hidden away for a while. It won't be for long, I'm sure. I'm sorry, but some of the time you will be locked in."

"It's so cold and I'm frightened and I want my mummy and daddy!" Kayla answered, beginning to cry again.

"Be brave, sweetheart, and I'll do my best for you," Nanny was whispering again. She obviously did not want Jim to hear her. "I wish I could explain. I'm a sort of prisoner here, too."

After she had eaten, Nanny Sue came back with a cup of tea and then told her to get ready for bed.

"But I don't have any washing things or PJ's," said Kayla, "and I have no clean clothes to wear tomorrow."

"I'll lend you some of my things so that you can wash, and tomorrow I'll try to get you what you need," answered her nanny.

When Kayla was ready for bed, she heard the key turn in the lock, and she knew she really was a prisoner. She felt very frightened. She had no idea where she was, only that she was a long way from home and somewhere out in the wilds. She thought of her parents and how frantic they would be when they realised she was missing. A big lump came in her throat, making it hard to swallow. She tried not to cry. Somehow, she knew it would make that man Jim mad if he heard her. She could hear muffled talking downstairs and later heard Jim and Nanny Sue come upstairs to the other bedroom. They were still talking a lot, and sometimes she heard Jim shout and swear. After a long time, Kayla fell asleep.

The next morning when she woke up, Kayla was confused. What was she doing in this strange room? She was so cold! Then she remembered all that had happened the day before. She wondered why she had been kidnapped. "Was Nanny Sue kidnapped too?" she wondered, because she had told her she was also a sort of prisoner.

There was a weird grinding noise, and the key turned in the lock. Kayla was relieved to see her old nanny's face and not that of the horrible man she had married.

"I need the bathroom," she said to Nanny Sue. She was stiff from being so cold in bed, and Nanny had to help her up and took her to the bathroom.

"I'm nine, not a baby," she said to Nanny Sue, hating to be followed everywhere.

"I know, sweetheart, but Jim said I must not let you go alone, and I dare not disobey him." Her nanny tried to smile, but it was a poor effort. Kayla looked at Nanny Sue and realised how thin she now was, and she had lots of bruises on her arms and deep shadows under her eyes. "You can come downstairs for breakfast, and there is a little camping gas stove which may help to keep us warm," she was told.

Kayla was glad to get out of the bedroom and followed her nanny downstairs. Jim was in the kitchen. He barely looked up when they entered. Nanny Sue had made some porridge, and it was hot and sweet. It made Kayla feel better. Then she made her some toast with Marmite, which had always been her favourite for breakfast.

Jim got up and glared at them both.

"I have to go and make a phone call. I won't be long. Don't even think about escaping. I would soon find you and my, how you would pay for it!" he threatened.

"Don't be so stupid, Jim. I am here to take care of Kayla, and that is what I will do. However, we need some shopping, and either you or I or both of us will have to get things for Kayla today," answered Nanny Sue.

Kayla was glad when she heard Jim leave the cottage. She was surprised because she didn't hear the car 'rev' up, but when she peered out of the window, there was no sign of it. She turned to her nanny. With that man out of the way, maybe she would get some answers!

Chapter Twelve

Nanny Sue came and sat on the horrid, dirty sofa beside her.

"What is going on, Nanny?" Kayla asked. "Why am I here and why are you a prisoner too? Please tell me while that horrible man is out."

"Yes, Kayla, I owe you an explanation. I hate to tell you because I know you love me and trust me. Even when you hear what I have to tell you, please know that I love you and am on your side. Your family made the decision to live in Dorset because they thought it would be safer for you. Your father is a very important scientist working for the government. There are other enemy governments who want to know what he is doing. He knew his life could be in danger and also yours and your mother's. That is why they took a house in a remote village. You were old enough not to need a nanny any more, so I had to find another job. I was quite upset about leaving you, for I had looked after you since you were a tiny baby; it was almost as if you were my own daughter. I felt so lost without you, and so one evening I went out to try and forget by drinking far too much alcohol to 'drown my sorrows' at a night club. It was there I met Jim. He made a fuss of me and began to ask me out. I dreamt that maybe one day I might get married and have my own little girl to love! He was very nice to me at first.

"Right from the start, he told me lots of lies. Now I know that he was only using me in order to kidnap you and ask a huge ransom from your parents and secret papers to sell to another government. If I had known that then, I would have gone straight to the police! As it was, he was sweet and kind and asked me to marry him. I agreed because I thought I loved him. He didn't want any fuss, just a quiet wedding in a registry office with a couple of his friends to be witnesses. I felt sad at not having a 'proper' white wedding with you as my bridesmaid, but sometimes things don't work out as you wish, and I was happy to marry Jim. We went to live in his flat, which was quite small and not very clean. I did my best to make it look like a home, keeping it clean and entertaining his friends. He would never allow my friends to come and not even allow me to write to them or phone them. Jim began to control my whole life. He also began to be cruel, and if he couldn't get his own way he would swear at me and even hit me. Then he told me of his plan. He had only courted me in order to kidnap you. He knew where I lived and that I had been your nanny and had been thinking of how he could meet me when I stupidly walked into the night club and into his trap! I blame myself for drinking as I did that night! Jim is a very evil man, and I am frightened of him. He even carries a gun, so I dare not disobey him.

That is why we have to do what he says, and please try to do what I tell you, so that you don't make him angry. That way, you won't get hurt."

Kayla looked at her nanny in total disbelief. She wondered how Nanny Sue could have been taken in by that horrible man! She reached out and squeezed her hand.

"That's a terrible story, Nanny. But how can we get out of this mess? I want to go home! Where is this place? Can't we run away together?"

"Jim chose this place because it is so far from everywhere. He has gone to a phone box now to phone his accomplice. I have no mobile, no money, nothing to help us get away. He will watch me like a hawk, because he knows I love you and I hate him for what he is doing. Now I had better wash up the dishes because he will be back any moment. Don't breathe a word of what I have told you," she warned.

Sure enough, Jim arrived back. He went into the kitchen and told Nanny Sue, "I have talked to 'Boss', and we will let them stew until this evening. Now, what is this shopping?"

Nanny Sue had made a list. Jim looked at it and frowned. "This is rubbish, what does she need all this for?"

Nanny Sue looked him in the eye and said, "There will be trouble if she is not well looked after. She is also very clever. She needs books and games to keep her happy and out of mischief. She needs to be warm in this freezing hovel." Her husband grudgingly agreed to her demands.

"When they pay up, there will be plenty of money, and we can disappear to somewhere warm," he muttered. "Lock the kid in the bedroom and I'll take you shopping!"

Once again Kayla was locked in the bedroom and left alone. For a while she sat and thought about all her nanny had told her. Then she got out her school reading book, but somehow she couldn't concentrate, even though it was a book she loved. As she sat on the bed, she began to think about her friend, Tess. She wondered how Omega the puppy was doing and how the lambs were thriving. Thinking about the lambs reminded her of the story Tess had told her about the lost sheep and the good shepherd who had searched for it until he found it, and how it was really a story that Jesus had told about Himself. She knew that Tess's family would talk to God about any problem. They called it 'praying'. Kayla wondered if God would hear her if she prayed now. She decided she would try.

"Dear God," she began, "things are in a real mess here. I don't really know you, but if you can help me, please, will you? I want to go back safely to my mum and dad. They will be terribly worried. Please let them know I am alright. I feel very sorry for Nanny Sue too. I am glad she is here with me. It would be much worse on my own, but this horrible man is controlling her and making her kidnap me. Please, please help us! I know you are good at finding lost sheep, so please let me get found! Amen."

After her prayer, Kayla felt a bit better. She did think God had heard and could help her. She picked up her book and this time was able to read it and enjoy it. It was quite a long time before she heard the car return, and Nanny Sue came up to the room with two big carrier bags. One had some clothes and toiletries and the other books and games. She gave her nanny a quick hug and thanked her.

"I am going to make us some lunch now, Kayla. Come down and help me, if you like," she said.

Kayla was pleased to be out of her 'prison' and glad to help. Jim was sitting in the small lounge reading the paper. Kayla couldn't help but see that the headline was 'Daughter of famous scientist kidnapped. There are fears for her life.' She felt tingles down her spine as she read that. Surely Nanny Sue wouldn't let anything happen to her; she had promised to take care of her!

Chapter Thirteen

A huge cloud of worry had descended on the Syding villages. There were police cars and policemen all over the place. The police went to every house asking questions. All the searches for Kayla had proved fruitless. The only clue the police had to work on was the information which Tim had been able to give them.

Tess was very upset. Kayla was her best friend. A policewoman had been sent to talk to her and asked lots of questions. She asked if Kayla had been unhappy at home or school and if she had ever talked of running away. She asked if she talked about her life when they lived in London.

It was hard to think back to all the chats she and Kayla had had. Once they had talked about 'never going with strangers' after a talk at school. She and Kayla hadn't really understood what the terrible things were, but they knew that some men tried to capture girls to do awful things to them and sometimes to boys too. They had promised each other that they would never talk to strange men and never take sweets from strangers or get in strange cars. Tess told this to the policewoman and also told her that Kayla often talked about her life at home. Sometimes Kayla felt sad because her parents were so busy and she had no one to play with, and she also had talked about the nanny who had looked after her from babyhood until they moved to the country. "Her name is Nanny Sue," said Tess, "and Kayla loved her very much. She said she was like a big sister to her. She had wanted her to come to the country when they moved, but her parents told her she was too big to have a nanny now. Anyway, her mum and dad would be around much more to take care of her themselves.

"We talked a lot about animals. Kayla loved to come to the farm. Her mum is allergic to animal fur, so she couldn't have any pets. We talked about all the books she read. In her house there is a whole room full of books. Kayla always said she was never bored because there was always a good book to read. She adores her mum and dad and is very proud of them. I am sure she would never run away."

The policewoman smiled at Tess and said she had been very helpful, but as soon as she had gone, Tess looked at her mum and began to cry.

"Mum, what if something terrible has happened to Kayla? She's so clever and pretty and kind. Our teacher says she will have a great future. Not like me. I can hardly read properly. All the letters get muddled up when I try. I am stupid and bottom of the class. I always wondered why she wanted to be my friend. Kayla always gets top marks at everything except art. Art isn't really that useful, is it? It's the only thing I can do."

Mrs Jenkins took her daughter on her lap and hugged her. She let her cry for a while, thinking to herself, "My Tess thinks she's stupid. How can I help her see that everyone is important and precious?"

When Tessa quietened down, her mum spoke to her.

"Tess, I know you think you are stupid because you find things like reading and maths hard and you compare yourself to Kayla. Why do you think that Kayla chose you to be her friend? It was because you are a very sweet, kind girl. The teachers at open evenings always tell me how hard you try and that you are always ready to help in any way you can, and also that you are gifted in art. You are not just good at art, you are brilliant for your age. God has made you a very special person, anything but stupid. When it comes to learning, we all do it at our own pace. Some people are very quick and others are slower, but they get there in the end. God wants you to know that you are special and His beloved child. He made you as you are, and you make Him sad when you wish you were different. If you were getting poor marks because you played around and didn't use the brain God gave you, then that is another matter. I never want you to say you are stupid again! You are gifted!"

This was quite a new thought to Tess, and she tried to believe it was true, for her mum always told her the truth. She had believed lies about herself for so long, it would not be easy to see herself as special to God.

All over the country, the police were looking for the car which Tim had spotted. Mr Jenkins had confirmed that Tim had a photographic memory as far as vehicles were concerned and he would have remembered the registration number accurately. It was mentioned on the news and television too. The vehicle had been traced to a man who was believed to live in London, who went by the name of 'Fred Cox' but was known to use other names too. The police were asking for him to come forward to 'help them with their enquiries.'

Detectives were staying with Kayla's parents. The phone had been wired up, hoping to trace any call that might come in demanding a ransom. Everyone was disappointed when the first day passed and there was no word from the kidnappers. The police had hoped that kidnapping in order to get money or secrets was the reason for Kayla's disappearance, but maybe it wasn't. Kayla's mother kept blaming herself because she was a few minutes late going to pick her daughter up from school that day. A strange phone call had come just as she was about to leave the house. The woman kept her talking about an article for the magazine, asking endless questions even though Kayla's mother had told the woman that she had to go and asked the caller to ring back in an hour.

At first Kayla's mum hadn't thought anything much about the phone call, but then she realised that it could have been a tactic to delay her from getting to school on time. When she told the detectives about this, they examined her phone and tried to trace the call. It proved to be genuine and was just a very tragic coincidence that had come at that moment.

It was a difficult case for the police. The most important thing for them was to find Kayla and return her to her parents, but they also had to protect her parents as her father was such an important man and worked on secret government work. The government department for which he worked were constantly on the phone too. If the secrets got into the wrong hands, then the national security could be at risk!

In the little cottage, Jim had finished reading his newspaper. He had waited long enough. It was now time for some action, he decided. Twenty-four hours had passed since they had kidnapped Kayla. Her parents had had time to think and maybe would be ready to do a deal. He needed a drink too! His accomplice had chosen this remote place for them to hang out, which was all very well for him—he was still in London and living his life as usual! Jim needed to find a pub and have a pint or two! No one in this area knew him, and although 'Boss' had told him this morning that the car had been spotted and the number plate had been shown on television and given out on the radio, he was sure none of the country yokels around here would notice it. It was fantastic as it could start without even revving up the engine!

He would find a lane in which to park it rather than a pub car park.

Jim looked at his wife and made a face. ‘Stupid woman!’ he thought. How easy it had been to deceive her! When all this was over and he was safely away in South America, he would tell her the truth. He couldn’t wait to see her face when he told her that he already had two wives, one whom he loved and the other whom he hated almost as much as her!

“I’m off out on business. Will be back at bedtime! Don’t wait up,” he said with an evil grin.

He locked Nanny Sue and Kayla in and took off.

Chapter Fourteen

Nanny Sue looked at Kayla and gave a sigh of relief.

"Let's make some supper," she said. "Afterwards we can play a game together until bedtime." They went into the makeshift kitchen and managed to cook a reasonable meal together. It was almost like old times, Kayla thought to herself, because when she was small, she had always liked cooking with her nanny. Then it had been little biscuits or cakes which she proudly presented to her parents when they came home. She tried to take her mind off the fact that she was kidnapped, trying to enjoy the meal and then beating Nanny Sue soundly at a game of Scrabble.

It was cold in the cottage, and the only way to keep warm in the evening was to go to bed. Kayla hated the thought of being locked in that little room all night. She suddenly had an idea.

"Nanny Sue," she asked, "please would you come and sleep in my room with me? I hate to be locked in alone, and it's so cold. It's at night that I feel most scared."

Nanny Sue's face brightened. "What a great idea! It will be a squash, but it will keep us both warm! I will lock us in from the inside, and then Jim cannot get to us when he returns. I expect he will have been drinking, and I would rather not be with him. Let's pretend it is a sleepover!"

That is what they did. Kayla was so thankful to be able to wash and get ready for bed on her own and glad to have some new PJ's to wear too. They were pretty, just the sort she would have chosen if she had been shopping. "Nanny Sue knows me well," she thought.

Just before they settled to sleep, Kayla remembered something. Since she had prayed to Jesus and thought about Him as the Good Shepherd looking for the lost sheep, she had felt calmer. She knew she should say thank you to Him. She quietly closed her eyes and whispered her 'thank you' before falling asleep. Her nanny lay beside her unable to get to sleep. How had she got herself into this mess? How would it all end? She thought she would probably be sent to prison for being an accomplice, albeit unwillingly, to the kidnapping.

After Jim left the cottage, he drove to the nearest village where there was both a phone box and a pub. He knew he should phone and make his ransom demand first. He had been given strict instructions by the man he called "Boss" who was the mastermind behind the kidnapping. He had been told to make the demands, not talking about anything except the ransom, the place of exchange and the time. Jim had been warned that most likely the police would be monitoring the call and trying to get the number of the phone box. Once it was all agreed, he was to bring the girl to the phone box, and Boss would take over from there. He and Nanny Sue were then to drive to a small aerodrome nearby and wait for Boss to come with the money and papers. A share of the money would be handed over to Jim, and he could make a hasty exit from the country. He had a passport in one of his three identities and tickets to Brazil in his pocket. The plan seemed foolproof!

Once in the village, Jim found the temptation to visit the pub first and have a couple of drinks irresistible. What harm would a couple of pints do? He thought to himself and decided that that is what he would do before phoning. The pub was warm and inviting. In the fireplace was a roaring wood fire, and he really needed to warm up after that cold cottage! Then he smelt the cottage pie that a customer was eating and decided he was also very hungry! An hour, a meal and several pints of beer later, he walked down the road to make his phone call.

When the phone rang at Kayla's home, the police told her father, "If it is the kidnapper, try to keep him talking as long as possible. Ask lots of questions to establish that Kayla is alright. Just try to stall him as long as possible before you agree to his demands. However, don't make him angry!"

With a shaky voice, Kayla's dad answered. Jim began his rehearsed speech asking for money and the secret papers. He was a bit slurred and hesitant in his speech, which gave Kayla's dad the chance to ask a few questions.

"Is my daughter alright?" he asked. "Is she eating properly? Are you looking after her?" He was struggling to know quite what he could ask to stall the kidnapper.

Jim seemed a bit confused by the questions and began to tell Kayla's dad that of course she was being looked after and they had even been shopping to buy her some pyjamas and toiletries.

The policeman beamed and encouraged Kayla's father. He was doing well! Suddenly, Jim remembered Boss's instructions and became angry. He made his demands again for the huge sum of money and the secret papers, telling Kayla's father a grid reference where he would find his daughter as soon as he had delivered the ransom.

"Don't think you can fool with me," he added, "and no police. I am armed and will not hesitate to pull the trigger on your kid if you try to outwit me!"

At this, Kayla's mum stifled a cry. Her father again tried to stall Jim by asking for the map grid reference once again so that he could write it down, then agreed to be at the place with the ransom at the time appointed the next day.

"Good! You did very well!" congratulated the detective. "You talked long enough for us to get the phone number. Now let's check that against the map reference number and get moving. We must warn the officers on the case that we know he is armed. You have done your part. Now it is our turn. Tomorrow morning we will escort you to the bank who has already been warned you may need a vast sum. You have prepared the 'dummy' secret papers. Hopefully, your daughter will be safe home tomorrow and the criminals under lock and key!"

After the phone call, Jim felt very pleased with himself. He thought he had managed it all very well. The scientist had not quibbled about the huge ransom or about giving up the secrets. All he wanted to know was that his daughter was safe. With a light heart, he started to walk back to the lane where the car was parked. At the last minute, he changed his mind and went back to The Black Bull Inn where he had eaten his supper. He sat by the roaring fire and settled down to enjoy a few more drinks. There was no hurry to go back to the freezing cottage in the middle of nowhere. He might as well enjoy the evening. Tomorrow would take him to a new country and a new life! After a few more drinks, he became drowsy and did not hear the sirens of the police cars. They had traced the phone box from which his call had been made and had begun to search the area. It wasn't long before Jim's car was found parked in the lane near the pub. The police suspected he might be in The Black Bull Inn but knew he could be armed and needed to take care. One patrol car stayed in the lane guarding the car.

There was no doubt about it, just as Tim had remembered; the registration number was EX 123 RIP.

Two plain clothes detectives made their way over to the pub. They only knew that the car belonged to Mr Fred Cox; they did not know for sure that the kidnapper operated under three names (or that he had three wives!). They decided to look around the car park first, and two young men came out and made their way to one of the cars. The detectives approached them, showing them their I.D. cards and asked them, "Are you local men?"

"Yes, sir," answered one of the guys. "Why do you ask?"

"We are looking for a man, possibly with a London accent. Is anyone in the pub this evening whom you do not know?"

"Yes, there is," answered the second guy. "Sitting by the fire and almost asleep is a man that I don't recognise, and I have lived in this village all my life! When he asked for a drink, he didn't sound from around these parts."

"Thank you for your help, lads," said the detective. They decided it was time to make a move. They went through the door and glanced quickly around and soon spotted Jim near the fire. He didn't look up when they entered, so they spoke first to the landlord. He confirmed that the man by the fire was a stranger who had been drinking heavily most of the evening, apart from about half an hour when he went out.

"That sounds like our man!" one detective said to the other. "Let's go for him!"

Jim was taken completely by surprise! He was so drowsy from all the drink that when the policeman confronted him and asked him if he was Fred Cox, he answered that he was, forgetting he was supposed to be Jim Clark! He was searched, the weapon found, then he was handcuffed and cautioned, much to the great interest of all the customers. Nothing as exciting as that ever occurred in their little village!

Chapter Fifteen

Jim was taken to the nearest large police station for questioning. He was so drunk that he didn't resist at all, but neither was he in much of a state to answer questions. When he had been searched, not only was he in possession of a gun, but also he had the phone number of Kayla's parents and the map grid reference in his pocket, all very incriminating evidence. The police found keys too in his pockets. Not only were there the keys for the car, but there was also a large, old-fashioned type of house key and a normal 'Yale' type of key. The car was driven away for forensics, while Jim was left in a cell to sober up.

Back in the cottage, Nanny Sue woke with a start. She heard knocking at the front door. When she looked at her watch, she couldn't believe it was seven in the morning! She had slept most of the night and had not heard Jim come in. Quickly, she grabbed her dressing gown and unlocked the door of Kayla's room and ran downstairs. Of course, she was also locked in! She went to the kitchen window and saw it was a couple of policemen at the door. She tried to open the window, but it was stuck. However, the police saw her and came over.

"We are doing a house to house search, looking for a nine-year-old girl. Please open the door so that we can talk to you," one said.

Nanny Sue answered, "Thank God! Kayla is here and quite safe, but the door is locked and we don't have a key."

"Don't worry," answered the policeman. "We'll try to get in. If we can't, we'll get some help. You are safe now. The kidnapper is in custody."

The police looked all around the cottage and decided they could get in through the back door without too much trouble. By this time Kayla was up and realising they were being rescued. She ran downstairs and hugged her nanny.

"We are safe. It's all over, Nanny Sue!" she said in delight.

"For you, dear," answered her nanny. "I am afraid I shall be arrested as a kidnapper and go to prison. At least you are safe, and that is what matters most."

Once the police were in the cottage, they were both told to get dressed and that they would be taken to the nearest police station where they could tell their story to the detectives. They were given warm blankets, which they wrapped around themselves as it was so cold, and were told they would be given breakfast when they arrived at the station. Kayla was glad of that because now that she was safe, she realised her tummy was rumbling because she was hungry. Everything had been left in the cottage for the forensic scientists to examine, even her school books!

They were greeted by two very kind policewomen and the detective inspector in charge of the case. The first thing that happened was that Kayla was allowed to speak to her parents, who had been told that she had been found unharmed and wanted reassurance. After they had eaten, Kayla was taken to another room to talk to the policewoman and even be examined by a doctor to make sure she had not been harmed in any way. She was a nice lady, and Kayla found it easy to tell her all about what had happened right from the moment she left the school gates.

Nanny Sue was taken to a different interview room, and a policewoman and a detective asked her many, many questions. She told them the entire long, sad story of how she had been tricked into a marriage in order to lead her husband and his accomplice 'Boss' to Kayla. She told them how she had had no idea at first of what was planned and how then she had been forced at gunpoint to comply. She admitted being party to kidnapping but said she had done all she could to look after Kayla throughout the ordeal and that she didn't care what happened to her so long as Kayla was safe. The relief of it all made Nanny Sue sob and sob and sob. She was quite distraught.

Having received Nanny Sue's confession, it confirmed what Jim had told them now that he had sobered up. There was another accomplice, 'Boss', and he was due to meet Kayla's father for the 'pick up'. So far the operation had gone brilliantly, but the detectives wanted to clear up the case completely by arresting Boss as well. They had to make careful plans for this.

Jim, when he realised what a mess he had made of things and that all his plans were ruined, decided to help the police. He knew he would be in for a long prison sentence and was intelligent enough to know that if he was really helpful then maybe it would be lessened. He told the detective inspector all about the plans Boss had made for the exchange and getaway. He even told them about his three identities and marriages.

As soon as it could be arranged, Kayla's parents were brought to be reunited with her. Until the last arrest had been made, the press were not allowed to know that she had been found. If the news was leaked out, then Boss might not turn up for the exchange.

How Kayla hugged her mum and dad! They were so relieved to see her safe and sound! However, the ordeal wasn't quite over. An hour or so before the time which had been arranged for the exchange, Kayla was taken with Nanny Sue to the place where she was supposed to 'be found'. It was in the telephone box, near the pub where Jim had been drinking and also near the small aerodrome where he was to make his getaway. Two armed policemen were hidden nearby just in case there was any trouble, and they had even given Nanny Sue an imitation, but most realistic, firearm!

Jim had been driven in his car to the aerodrome and then locked in, and his hands were cuffed and the car demobilised. Everything had to look exactly as it would have done had the plan gone ahead. The police knew that Jim was really only a minor criminal. The real international kidnapper and spy was 'Boss'. They didn't want to lose this 'big fish'!

The grid reference was close to the red phone box where Nanny Sue and Kayla were waiting. Although it was a chilly February day and they had a long wait, Kayla now felt she was acting in a play, excited to be part of the action. Maybe she was still in real danger, but she didn't feel it. She could feel that Nanny Sue was nervous and tried to calm her down. Suddenly, the phone rang, making them both jump out of their skins! They didn't know this was part of the plan. After about three rings, Nanny Sue picked it up and said, "Hello."

"Good," said a voice. "Just wanted to check that you and the girl are in place. Don't let the kid run to her father until he has given me the goods. When you see me get in the car with the ransom, you send her running and then you run to meet Jim at the plane. Got that?"

"Yes, Boss," said Nanny Sue quietly and put the receiver down. She felt for the imitation gun in her pocket, somehow glad that she had it. What a good thing they had come to wait in the right place!

At the appointed hour, Kayla's father drove up and waited at a crossroads. Kayla could see him there. She knew the detectives were hidden in different places, ready to pounce. In her heart she felt sure it would all go to plan. She had asked God to take care of her daddy too. On the other side of the crossroads, a fancy-looking car approached. It stopped, but the engine kept running. A tall, thin man wearing a balaclava that covered all but his eyes came over to her daddy. It was like something on television! The man spoke to him and then pointed to where she was in the telephone box. Her father nodded and went into his car and took out a briefcase. He opened it and was showing the man what was inside when suddenly from all sides of the crossroads policemen appeared. Some even had guns! They arrested Boss, handcuffed him and searched him for any weapons, then took him away. The policewoman who was looking after Kayla came to the phone box and told her she could now go and stay with her father, but Nanny Sue was handcuffed and taken to the police car. Kayla felt sad about that and gave her a big hug as she got into the car and thanked her for taking such good care of her.

"Things will be alright, you'll see," she said. "I will pray for you. I know God hears our prayers."

When the news reached Little and Much Syding, the vicar ran to the church and rang the bell! Everyone was so relieved and so thankful that God had answered their prayers. There was a huge fuss, and the press everywhere wanted to take pictures and ask questions, but the villagers didn't like that and wouldn't talk to them. In the end, all they got was one photograph of Kayla with her mum on one side and her dad on the other going to church for a special service to say 'thank you to God' that it had all ended so well.

The minister explained to the congregation that Kayla had been kidnapped so that wicked people could extract a huge ransom for her release. He went on to tell everybody about the greatest ransom that had ever been paid and called it the 'ransom of our souls'. Many of the villagers wondered what he was talking about, but he continued to explain that all people were taken captive by God's enemy, Satan, after Adam and Eve sinned in the Garden of Eden. People's sin is what separates them from God, and the only way for them to be rescued and brought back to God was for the greatest ransom of all to be paid. The death of Jesus was the ransom price. When Jesus died on the cross, he paid that price with his own life. He himself became the ransom for us. The price of our sins was paid and because of that, when people say sorry to God and ask for His forgiveness, it is possible for them to be free again and return to a relationship with God. Everyone was very quiet as they thought about that.

The minister urged people to turn back to God while they had time. He reminded them of the urgency of the search for Kayla and that there is an urgency to return to God without delay, for the ransom has been paid. There was no need to stay as a prisoner of Satan the enemy any longer; the Lord was waiting with His arms open for them to say sorry and to return!

It was a powerful message that made the congregation think and say thank you not only for Kayla's safe return but also for the ransom which Jesus had paid for everyone.

it right, I was a bit muddled, but I did realise that I was like a lost sheep, and I asked Jesus to help people find me and to take care of Mummy and Daddy. I know God heard my prayer, and I felt less panicky and stopped crying all the time. I was able to be calm and somehow trust that God would make it all come right in the end." Kayla paused for a few moments. "I felt so angry with Nanny Sue! You know I would never have got into a car with a stranger, but Nanny Sue had hugged me, and I was so excited to see her and she sort of pushed me into the car without me noticing who was driving. When we were alone and she told me her story, I realised she had been tricked too. She did all she could to look after me. I told her I had prayed, and I will go on praying for her. I know it will be months before the trial, but I pray the judge will be kind to her. Do you know what Mummy told me? The man she married, Jim, had already married two other women using different names. In fact, she isn't legally married to him at all, and I am so glad about that!"

"Let's go and see Omega," suggested Tess. The two girls ran from the lambing barn to another outhouse where Pickles the Labrador bitch was looking after her puppies. They were growing so fast, even Omega, the little runt. As soon as Tess came in, Omega ran over to her, already recognising her as his mistress.

"Mummy said she will not sell him, but he can be ours. We will share him. I know you cannot have a dog at home, but when he is big enough and had all his injections, you can take him out for walks and he will always protect you."

Kayla gave her friend a big hug. She had always wanted a dog! Now she had half-shares in one.

"Can I ask you something else?" said Kayla. "Could you ask the rest of the Syding Wildlife Society if I could be a member, too? I should so like to join a club. I wanted to join the Brownie Guides, but mum says Dorchester is too far away. She doesn't like to let me out of her sight anymore! She did say I could stay on at school for Bible club each week, and I'm glad of that."

"I am sure the gang will let you," said Tess. "In fact, I shall ask the 'Two T's' and the twins tomorrow at church. I know Paul and Tim will not mind."

Tess was as good as her word and asked everyone the next day if Kayla could join the club. Nobody minded. In fact, they were all pleased and said they would have a meeting the next Saturday morning. They decided to meet as usual at the castle so that they could take Kayla on a tour of the river, lake and copse. Kayla was really pleased, and Mrs Jenkins invited her to come on the Friday after school for another sleepover if her mum agreed. Everyone wanted to help her forget the horrible experience she had been through.

Towards the end of February, the weather really began to change, and it cheered everyone to think that spring was on the way! There were other changes too. The archaeologists

Jesus came to earth to save people and took the punishment they deserved for sinning by His dying on the cross instead of them. If they asked Him to forgive them, then they could begin a new life as a child in God's family.

When that happens, there is a big party in heaven, just like at the end of the lost sheep story where it tells us that the shepherd is so glad that the sheep has been found that he calls his friends together to have a party. Kayla re-read the story, and she began to understand. Yes, she truly believed that God had heard her prayer and helped her to be found when she was a prisoner in the cottage, but now she understood that she had gone her own way and run away from Jesus, the Good Shepherd, and in her own simple way, she said sorry to Him and asked Him to find her and carry her home into His family. She told Jesus she wanted to learn more about Him and always belong to Him.

When everyone was chatting and enjoying drinks and biscuits and then playing a 'lost sheep' game, she sat and read the story over and over again. Tess came and asked her if she was alright and if she wanted to join in the game, but she smiled at her friend and explained that she wanted to talk to Jesus about being her 'Good Shepherd'. Tess understood and let her go on reading. What a great friend Tess was, thought Kayla. Just the very best!

Chapter Seventeen

It was very quiet at the castle after the archaeologists had left. Theo's mum had very few enquiries for bed and breakfast. Not many people wanted to take short holiday breaks in February. She decided maybe it was time to spring clean. Tyler's mum Betty came to help her, and everywhere seemed chaotic. Theo looked after his chickens and ducks as usual but otherwise spent a lot of the time in the swimming pool, which he had begged his mother to keep open, as there was a county schools' swimming gala coming up and he was representing his school in the under-thirteen team doing freestyle, relay and also butterfly. He wasn't that confident with butterfly stroke, but no one else was willing to enter, so he said he would. It was easy for him to practice, and sometimes Seb would swim against him, giving him some competition, with Flick timing them both. It was hard work, but he loved it. He always felt refreshed after a good swim, even if his muscles ached.

He had been practising one day after school and then climbed the steps to his room and was listening to some music when his mobile rang. It was his mum. She found climbing all those steps too hard after spring cleaning all day.

"There's a phone call for you from the Dorchester Museum," she told him.

"I'll be right down," Theo answered and ran down the hundred stairs and into the kitchen.

"Hello, Theo," the curator said. "I have your New Testament ready for you, and have found out a bit of history. When would you like me to bring it over?"

"I'll just ask my mum," answered Theo and told her what the curator had told him. They decided that Friday after school would be a good time, so it was arranged.

Theo sent an email to Pip to inform him and say he was welcome to come back down, but it would mean sharing the turret because of spring cleaning. Much as Pip wanted to come, he emailed back to say he wasn't able to but asked Theo to be sure and email all the news. Tyler, however, was excited about the curator coming, and so was Paul. Both Seb and Flick decided to come straight home after school too.

The curator arrived with the New Testament carefully wrapped and also with a folder of papers. Everyone sat around the kitchen table waiting to hear what he had to say.

"As you know, your castle started as a Tudor manor house, completed around 1490. It was quite splendid for its time, and you know it had a great hall, kitchens and cellars. Around it was a moat, which was filled in about 200 years later. Over the centuries, it has been added to and remodelled. The chapel you discovered must have been part of the original building, though it may not have been built for that purpose. The small arched doorways into it are definitely Tudor in origin. The window looks a slightly later addition.

"At the time the manor was built, it was constructed for Sir Frederick Mountaley. He was descended from the Normans and was a very rich landowner. All the farms in the area once belonged to him, as well as both villages. They were much smaller, of course. He was known as a brave and good man, and the lions at the end of the drive are also from the original house, as he was known to have a 'lion's heart'.

"In 1525 William Tyndale translated and printed his first version of the New Testament in English. It was a very brave thing to do because, although Martin Luther had stood out against the current teaching of the Roman Catholic Church, here in England that church was totally dominant and outlawed Tyndale's New Testament. This was because his translation interpreted texts in such a way that it went against some of that church's teaching. It also meant that ordinary people could read the Bible for themselves and not only the priests.

"William Tyndale had to live in exile in Europe in countries in which people were beginning to read and accept the new understanding of the Gospel. These people were what we now call 'Protestants'. Tyndale continued to translate many Old Testament books. In fact, his work is the basis of what later became the 'King James Bible'. Tyndale was executed for translating the scriptures! He was strangled and then his body burned! He was a great reformer who became a martyr for his faith.

"The power of both the Roman Catholic Church and the state was so great in those days that a ban was passed condemning Tyndale's translations, and any which were found in England had to be burned.

"This New Testament you found is one of the original copies. It is very rare and precious. Investigation of Sir Frederick relates that he became one of the very early Protestants but had to practice his faith in secret. That is why the chapel is in the cellar and also is so plain. The Protestants did not want ornate places of worship like the churches they were used to. They wanted to read the Bible for themselves and find out the truth about God and salvation from its pages.

"After King Henry Tudor was enthroned, but before the reformation began in 1534, sadly your brave knight was executed for his faith. It appears the secret chapel was bricked up at that time and has not been used since. It would explain the wonderful condition of this New Testament."

When the curator had finished, everyone sat for a moment in silence. There was so much to take in. Finally Sally, Theo's mum, spoke, maybe what they all were thinking.

"To think that after all these hundreds of years we have come to live here and have not only discovered this old chapel and the Tyndale New Testament, but we have also discovered the same faith and the same salvation which Jesus came to bring!"

She explained to the curator how they had come to live in the castle, a very wealthy family who just lived to make money and please themselves. Then everything had fallen apart when her husband had left her and the children. They had to choose whether to sell up or to all work together and make the castle into a business in order to pay off the mortgage. Their whole lifestyle changed, but they also, one by one, had been coming to know God in a real way. Theo's mum said how it made her feel very humble to think she was in some little way following in the footsteps of a martyr.

The curator gave them all the information he had gathered, and Seb thought he would make it a project to make a book about it all. For the time being, Sally felt the Tyndale New Testament should be put into a safe in the bank until she had time to decide what should happen to it. The 'Two T's' were more than ever determined to make the old chapel a 'prayer space' again. Theo knew Pip would come and help them, as well as the archaeologists when they returned. He understood that it was a 'national treasure' and that any restoration would have to be supervised carefully, but he longed for it to be used once more as a chapel. He just hoped it wouldn't take years and years!

Titles available in the Syding Adventures

CARAVANS AND CASTLES (1)
Mary Weeks Millard
ISBN 978-1-84625-364-5

PIRATES AND PRISONERS (2)
Mary Weeks Millard
ISBN 978-1-84625-365-2

SUNSHINE AND SNOWSTORMS (3)
Mary Weeks Millard
ISBN 978-1-84625-366-9

ROMANS AND RANSOMS (4)
Mary Weeks Millard
ISBN 978-1-84625-367-6

LIVE WIRES AND LOBSTER POTS (5)
Mary Weeks Millard
ISBN 978-1-84625-368-3

Coming soon in the Syding Adventures

VIKINGS AND VISITORS (6)
Mary Weeks Millard
ISBN 978-1-84625-369-0

HOLIDAYS AND HIJACKINGS (7)
Mary Weeks Millard
ISBN 978-1-84625-370-6